TWO KINDS OF POWER
An Essay on Bibliographical Control

BY
PATRICK WILSON

UNIVERSITY OF CALIFORNIA PRESS
BERKELEY, LOS ANGELES, LONDON

UNIVERSITY OF CALIFORNIA PUBLICATIONS
LIBRARIANSHIP: 5

UNIVERSITY OF CALIFORNIA PRESS
BERKELEY AND LOS ANGELES
CALIFORNIA

UNIVERSITY OF CALIFORNIA PRESS, LTD.
LONDON, ENGLAND

ISBN: 0-520-03515-1
© 1968 BY THE REGENTS OF THE UNIVERSITY OF CALIFORNIA
CALIFORNIA LIBRARY REPRINT SERIES EDITION, 1978

CONTENTS

	Introduction	1
I.	The Bibliographical Universe	6
II.	Describing and Exploiting	20
III.	Relevance	41
IV.	Bibliographical Instruments and Their Specifications	55
V.	Subjects and the Sense of Position	69
VI.	Indexing, Coupling, Hunting	93
VII.	Consultants and Aids	114
VIII.	Reliability	125
IX.	Adequacy and Bibliographical Policy	132

INTRODUCTION

THE WORLD is full of writings. In libraries, archives, offices, and attic trunks is an enormous and rapidly increasing mass[1] of written material of all sorts, the products of learning and imagination and speculation, of observation and painstaking record keeping, of public and private business. Some of the writings are of lasting interest, representing the cores of civilizations, bodies of literature and law, religion and philosophy, theories about the world, and recipes for successful action. Most are only of passing interest to anyone, despite their being records or traces of human activity; not all of our history is worth remembering. The endless folders of business correspondence may never again need to be referred to; the angry letters to editors may be forgotten. Yesterday's newspaper and last year's popular novel might not be much missed if they were never found again, and perhaps only half a dozen people will ever again care to look at the latest papers in entomology or Romance philology. But almost any piece of writing might be of at least temporary interest and value to someone.

How can the valuable be kept from oblivion? How can a man be sure of finding, in the great mass of writings, good and bad, pedestrian and extraordinary, the writings that would be of value to him? In some remote Golden Age, a sufficiently intelligent, industrious, and wealthy man might have discovered, acquired, and mastered all of the writings, or at least all of the "public" writings, that his society had produced or acquired from other producers, and so have become acquainted with all those of even remote interest to him. Now there is too much for any one to master, so much that is it difficult to sort out that which one would like to master from that which one cannot be bothered to try to master. Discovery of the valuable in the mass of the mostly worthless or uninteresting is a major ingredient in the problem of bibliographical control. But there are other ingredients in that complex problem, and it is our job to attempt to understand them all, as best we can.

The attempt might be thought needless, for do we not already understand what bibliographical control is, how it is attained, and why it is desired? The words "bibliographical control" are used freely enough by people who must know what they are talking about. But understanding has many va-

---

[1] For critical comments on an earlier version of this addition to the mass, I am grateful to Professors J. P. Danton and M. E. Maron; for advice and encouragement I am deeply indebted to Professor R. C. Swank, Dean of the School of Librarianship.

rieties and nuances; there are ways and ways of knowing what one is talking about, of understanding the notions one employs and the things we discuss by employing those notions. If a term is familiar to us and comfortable in use, we may say, not without reason, that we understand it; if an activity is one we freely engage in, if a goal is one we know how to pursue, we may properly claim to understand the activity and realize what we are doing in pursuing the goal. But we may also say that until we make clear and explicit to ourselves, by reflection on our activities and goals, what it is we know and how that knowledge is related to the rest of our knowledge, we do not *fully* understand or fully realize what we have been doing and pursuing.

So our attempt here will be to make explicit what we may already know about bibliographical control, and to say how that knowledge is related to the rest of our knowledge. Such attempts have the slightly paradoxical quality of being more interesting when failures than when successes; if such an attempt is successful, what is said must seem obviously true, while where it is most interesting, it is most likely to be false. This is not quite correct, however, for attempts at understanding almost invariably discover obscurities and unsuspected difficulties, which one tries not merely to disclose but to eliminate. Analysis is not in practice separable from criticism, nor elucidation from reform and rebuilding. But a little clarification in one place is likely only to expose further obscurities and difficulties in neighboring places, and there is some truth in the claim that we cannot clarify anything unless we clarify everything. Since we cannot manage that, we must be content with relative clarity and a bit of precarious understanding.

In what follows, then, we shall attempt an analysis or clarification of the notion of bibliographical control. We shall have to say what that control might be exercised over, and to try to describe the sorts of exercise that would count as exercises of bibliographical control. We shall have to consider the sorts of instruments and arrangements that might be employed in such exercises, and to isolate the features of these on which their utility would depend. We shall have to ask how one would estimate the amount of control a man had, and how one would decide when and in what directions control should be extended. Two notions will be singled out for particular discussion, largely critical: the notion of relevance, central to the study of information retrieval, and the notion of the subject of a writing, central to library practice. These are not the only notions we shall encounter

Introduction 3

that deserve extended examination, but they are prominent among the deserving. The sum of our discussion is not meant to be the establishment of a single thesis or claim; bibliographical control is the one big thing we would like to illuminate, but not by the means of establishing one big claim. The discussion does not include the formulation of practical programs of action or the description of new devices or methods; we shall be concerned, as it were, with the "anatomy and physiology" of a power, rather than with cures and hygienic regimes. No doubt cures and regimes are needed, but so is clarity about goals in the search for cures and regimes, and about the bases of their evaluation.

What we see as problems of control, others have seen as problems of organization.[2] Organization is, we might say, a structural notion, while control is a functional notion; organization is something that things have or are given, control is something we have or wield over things. In theory the two notions are distinct, but in practice one cannot talk of control without talking of organization, for one of the chief ways in which we control things is by taking advantage of the organization they exhibit. Of course we organize people as well as things, and a group of people might under some circumstances constitute a bibliographical organization, one of the purposes of which was to produce or exercise bibliographical control. The ways in which people, organized and unorganized, contribute to other people's bibliographical control will concern us as much as the ways in which the organization of things contributes to control. But not all the problems of bibliographical organization are equally important in a discussion of bibliographical control, and many of the questions discussed in the enormous literature of bibliographical organization will go unnoticed here.

As we cannot avoid discussing bibliographical organization, so we cannot avoid discussing bibliography. But, though it might seem to be otherwise, there is no necessary connection, though of course many factual connections, between bibliographical control and bibliography, in either of the two main senses of the word "bibliography." That word is a name for a kind of work, namely the making of lists of a certain sort; it is also the name of a

---

[2] Verner W. Clapp's "The Role of Bibliographic Organization in Contemporary Civilization," in *Bibliographic Organization,* ed. Jesse H. Shera and Margaret E. Egan (Chicago, 1951), pp. 3–23, illustrates nicely the difference in point of view between the two ways of treating the difficulties.

kind of study, primarily the study of the history of books and printing.³ The results of the study may be presented in the form of a list, the study might even be undertaken in order to make a proper list. But one can make lists without being a student of the history of books and printing, and can be a student of that history without ever making lists. One may acquire a measure of bibliographical control through one's knowledge of the history of books and printing, but that is by no means the only way of acquiring such control. Further, though the existence of various sorts of lists may confer on those to whom they are available a measure of control, they may fail to do so, and may not have been meant to do so; nor are lists the only instruments of control. We shall not, as others have done,⁴ build the notion of bibliography into that of bibliographical control, the connection between the two being contingent rather than necessary, a matter of fact rather than of meaning.

Finally, the relationships between the organization and control of writings and the organization and control of knowledge and information will inevitably enter our story, for writings contain, along with much else, a great deal of mankind's stock of knowledge and information. Bibliographical control is a form of power, and if knowledge itself is a form of power, as the familiar slogan claims,⁵ bibliographical control is in a certain sense power over power, power to obtain the knowledge recorded in written form. As writings are not simply, and not in any simple way, storehouses of knowledge, we cannot satisfactorily discuss bibliographical control as simply control over the knowledge and information contained in writings. But the concepts employed in attempts to theorize about information stor-

---

³ This oversimplifies considerably. But there is no easy way of sorting out the various pursuits which go under the names of analytical, critical, descriptive, historical, textual, systematic bibliography. It seems best to take Arundell Esdaile's statement, in his *A Student's Manual of Bibliography* (London, 1931), p. 13, that bibliography is an art and a science with some seriousness, and identify the art with the making of lists, the science with the study of books as physical objects, a study that is primarily an historical one. The science, when applied in the exercise of the art, may result in the production of bibliographies that are "descriptive" or "critical"; but we are uninterested in a typology of bibliographies, and of the branches of the study called "bibliography." For a brief description of three of those branches, see Fredson Bowers, *Bibliography and Textual Criticism* (Oxford, 1964), pp. 24–28.

⁴ See *Bibliographical Services: Their Present State and Possibilities of Improvement*, The UNESCO/Library of Congress Bibliographical Survey (Washington, D.C., 1950), p. 1: "*Bibliographic control* is defined to mean the mastery over written and published records which is provided by and for the purposes of Bibliography. ('Bibliographic control' is synonymous with 'effective access through bibliographies.'...)"

⁵ Francis Bacon, *Novum Organum*, Book I, Aphorism 3: "Human knowledge and human power meet in one, for where the cause is not known the effect cannot be produced."

Introduction 5

age and retrieval are inevitably concepts of greater or lesser importance to our study; the conceptual inventories of the studies of bibliography and of information storage and retrieval overlap largely if they do not coincide.

Our age is by no means the first to see the many writings as being too many, as a plethora and hence as a problem, nor the first to look for remedies. The history of bibliography and librarianship is not a short one. But "records management" and "information retrieval" are of wider concern than ever before, and technological innovations seem to promise new remedies, or to offer the ingredients of possible remedies. There is less of conceptual innovation in most remedial proposals than enthusiasts and promoters think, but the impressive technology is undeniable. But technology tells us neither what is worth aiming at (or away from), nor what is a satisfactory degree of progress toward our elected goals. That we must discover or decide for ourselves; and that is best done with the greatest possible clarity about alternative goals and the intrinsic difficulties in their pursuit.

Chapter I

THE BIBLIOGRAPHICAL UNIVERSE

To have bibliographical control over a collection of things is to have a certain sort of power over those things: what things, and what sort of power, it is our business to discover or decide. Let us ask first what are the things over which one might have bibliographical control. A possible, and commonsense, answer would be simply "books"; another possible, and ultra-sophisticated, answer would be "items of information." Both these answers are unsatisfactory, for different reasons. Let us first consider a third answer and return later to the reasons the first two answers will not do. Let us say that the bibliographical universe, the totality of things over which bibliographical control is or might be exercised, consists of writings and recorded sayings. The universe of writings and recorded sayings includes items of radically different sorts, and our first task is to make quite clear what are the different varieties of inhabitants of that universe.

A man writes a poem, a letter to a friend, a report on an investigation; he spends a certain amount of time, a few minutes or many, at consecutive work or work spread out over many days, constructing a particular linguistic object, a piece of language. When he has finished, that is, when he has decided to call the piece of work complete, the result is a sequence of words and auxiliary symbols, generally but not always written or typed on a page. What he has done can be described in many ways, of which the most important ones for us are these: he has composed or invented a *work*, a poem or letter or report; he has ordered certain words into a certain sequence and so produced a *text*; he has produced marks or inscriptions on some material that constitute an *exemplar* of the text. The three descriptions are not independent, for he could have produced no work without producing some text, and could have produced no text without producing some permanent or transitory exemplar of that text. But the descriptions are by no means equivalent, for the work produced is not the text produced, nor is the text produced the exemplar produced. The three descriptions mention items of quite distinct varieties.

The relation of exemplar to text is a familiar one, but worth rehearsing nevertheless.[1] A text, a sequence of words and auxiliary symbols, is an abstract entity, like the words of which it is composed; its exemplars are of two distinct sorts, which we can call "performances" and "copies." If I recite a poem, I utter sounds that are instances of particular patterns or "types." My utterance is an event, or series of events, taking a certain length of time and occurring in a certain locality. But the pattern or "type" of which I produce an instance is not the sort of thing of which we can say that it takes a certain time or that it is anywhere at all. A book in which that same poem is printed is a physical object, weighing so much and taking up so much space. But the text of which the book contains an exemplar is no physical object, has no weight and occupies no space. If we were to set about counting the things to be seen and heard in the world, we might count so many books containing the text of that poem and so many recitations of that poem, but we would not also count the text of the poem, for it is not something that could be seen or heard in addition to the various events that are its performances and the various objects that are, or contain, its copies.

The events and objects that are performances and copies of a text may be of the most diverse sorts. I can recite a text, "say" it in the language of the deaf-mute, write it in sand, or trace letters on the surface of a pond. A text can be written, typed, printed, recorded on tape or phonograph record or sound film; a sign-language performance might be filmed. Most importantly, a text can be stored up in my memory, or in the "memory" of an electronic device, in such a way as to allow the production of further performances or further copies of the text. It is perhaps straining language a bit to speak of a text stored up in one's memory as a copy of the text. But as it is a quasi-permanent representation of the text, differing from other, written or printed, copies in not being directly observable, but not differing in that respect from copies on tape or phonograph record, there seems no harm in so extending the sense of "copy."

The distinction between work and text may also be familiar, but it is less easy to make with any precision.[2] Let us see, in the first place, why such a

---

[1] The relation of text to exemplar is that of "type" to "token," in the familiar terminology of C. S. Peirce in *Collected Papers*, IV (Cambridge, Mass., 1933), sect. 537. "Exemplar," the word I use in preference to "token" or "replica," is perhaps unfortunate, in that it can mean either archetype or instance; it is of course the second of these senses that the word bears in this discussion.

[2] See also Eva Verona, "Literary Unit versus Bibliographical Unit," *Libri*, 9 (1959), 79–104. In the *Anglo-American Cataloging Rules* (North American Text) (Chicago: American Library Association, 1967), the distinction of work and text appears most clearly in the section on Uniform Titles (chap. 4), but is implicit everywhere. See note 5 below.

distinction seems called for. Suppose a novelist produces a text, and suppose we claim that his novel, his work of literature, is simply that very text, that particular sequence of words. Suppose a translation of the novel is now made, say into Russian. Could a Russian who read only the translation be said to have read our author's work, or to be acquainted with his novel? Properly speaking, he could not, for he would have read no exemplar of the text that the author produced, and we are assuming the novel to be the text he produced. But this conclusion is contrary to our customary and perfectly sensible opinions. A copy of a translation of a work, we would naturally say, is a copy of that work. We would not say of a set of volumes labeled *The Works of Schopenhauer* that the volumes were incorrectly labeled simply because they contained no German texts. A copy of a translation of a poem may not, for special reasons, be counted as a copy of the poem;[3] but a copy of a translation of a novel or a history is surely a copy of the novel or the history.

Let us take another sort of case. A text having been produced, further slightly altered texts may in the course of time be produced, derived from the first but differing from it in various ways. Copyists will make mistakes, compositors introduce changes unnoticed by proofreaders, malicious editors emend and delete. There may finally be dozens of slightly different texts, all claiming the same title, all claiming to be "what the author wrote." Suppose that, as commonly happens, we are unsure which, if any, of the surviving texts is identical with the text originally produced by the author. If we identify the work produced with the text originally produced, we shall have, in such cases, to say that we do not know whether we are acquainted with the work; we shall have to deny acquaintance with *Hamlet,* or at least admit that we do not know whether we are acquainted with it or not. For all we know, we are only acquainted with a text that more or less resembles the text that is *Hamlet*. But this consequence, though not impossible to sustain, is paradoxical; our natural opinion is that we are certainly acquainted with *Hamlet,* though perhaps not acquainted with exactly the same text or texts as were Shakespeare's contemporaries.[4]

---

[3] A translation of a poem need not itself be a poem, so its copies would not be copies of poems. On the other hand, a translation of a poem may indeed be a poem; but it will not be the same poem as that of which it is a translation, and so its copies not copies of that poem. This is all a consequence of the fact (or what I would be willing to defend as a truth) that poems are "made out of words" in a rather different way from that in which non-poems are constructed of words.

[4] Since a text is a sequence of words and auxiliary symbols, completely defined by contents and order of elements, a single alteration produces a new text. Our ordinary beliefs reflect

The Bibliographical Universe

Still another sort of case argues the utility of the distinction of work and text. A writer may, in the course of his work, produce several different texts that he himself considers different versions of the same work, or different stages or drafts of one work. In the ordinary case he will finally declare one of those different texts to be authoritative, the text he wishes to have made public; but this might not happen, and in any case his audience might prefer versions other than the one he declared authoritative. If we were acquainted only with an early, unauthorized, version of a poem, we would have, without the distinction of work and text, to say that we were simply acquainted with a different work. Again, a writer may revise a text after it has been made public; in one of the several senses of the word "edition," he may produce revised editions of a text. Must we say that each different text is a different work, or may not two people, each of whom has read a different edition of a text, claim familiarity with the same work? The latter is clearly preferable.

The upshot is that there is sufficient reason for not identifying a work produced with a particular text produced; the relation of text to work must be a looser one than that of strict identity. There may be several, or many, texts that are all equally texts of the same work. If pressed to answer the question "But what, exactly, is a work, if it is not to be identified with any particular text?," we might answer by saying that a work simply is a group or family of texts, and that for a text to be a text *of* a particular work is the same thing as for it to be a member of a certain family. The production of a work is clearly not the writing down of all the members of the family, but is rather the starting of a family, the composing of one or more texts that are the ancestors of later members of the family.[5] There are no doubt other pos-

---

our notion that some alterations change the text "essentially" and others do not; the problem is that our notions of "essentiality" are to vague to be of much use.

[5] Something like this suggested view of authorship is necessary to save the *Anglo-American Cataloging Rules* from complete absurdity. In the section headed "Works with Authorship of Mixed Character" we read: "When different persons or bodies [corporate, not physical] have contributed to the intellectual or artistic content of a work by performing different kinds of functions (e.g., writing, adapting, illustrating, translating, editing, authorizing, etc.) the authorship is mixed in character and divided in responsibility" (op. cit., p. 23). Taken at face value, this suggests a wholly novel view of authorship. Whereas one had thought Shakespeare the author of *Hamlet*, since he wrote it, on this view one could become *partly* its author by illustrating an edition of it. Similarly, all the editors and translators of *Hamlet* would share in the authorship of *Hamlet*. This offends our ordinary sense of what it means to be an author. But the editors and translators of *Hamlet* have produced texts which we recognize to belong to the *Hamlet*-family, and so do share responsibility for extending that family beyond its first member or members. (Illustrators produce no new texts, but provide accompaniments for particular editions, that is, sets of copies, of some text.) The author starts a family, editors and translators continue it.

sible ways of elucidating the notion of a work, but this one will do for our purposes.

There is, however, a difficulty about the notion of a work, a difficulty that troubles library cataloguers and bibliographers if no one else. It is, simply, that there is no satisfactory general rule by reference to which one can sharply distinguish texts that are from those that are not texts of a given work. In terms of families of texts, there is no satisfactory general rule by reference to which family membership can be determined. A text once produced can collect, in time, a perfect swarm of parasites of different sorts: not only different versions made by the original producer, and "literal" translations, but, depending on the sort of work concerned, "free" translations, "free" paraphrases, bowdlerized versions, abridgments and rearrangements, critical editions, variorum editions, texts in which "mistakes" are corrected, texts "brought up-to-date" long after the author's death, commentaries in which some version of the original text is embedded, and so on almost indefinitely.

The impossibility of stating a general rule by reference to which family members could be distinguished from other sorts of derivatives of an original text can be shown, I think, merely by reflection on the problem of evaluating translations.[8] A translation must preserve the sense of its original, and it is not hard to imagine, or find, instances of texts claiming to be translations of such and such a work, but bearing so little resemblance to the original, preserving so little of the sense of the original, as to be "no translation at all." But there is no imaginable way of saying precisely how much of the sense of the original must be preserved, for a putative translation really to *be* a translation of some text. Again, we can imagine preparing a version of an old work, in the course of which we alter a word here and there, in the interests of greater intelligibility. Obviously we can, by successive alterations, finally produce a text differing in every particular from the original. This will surely be no text of the original; but at what point did we cease to produce modified versions of the original work, and begin to produce versions of a new work? Of course there is no way of saying, except arbitrarily.

---

[8] The *Anglo-American Cataloging Rules* instruct one to "Enter a translation of a work under the author of the original work," but "If the translation involves adaptation or is described as a 'free' translation, however, treat it as an adaptation" and so list it under the name of the translator. But no guidance is given for recognizing that a translation has "involved adaptation," and none for treatment of translations that are, but do not describe themselves as being, "free" translations.

The Bibliographical Universe

There is no general rule by which one could calculate that a text was too corrupt, too poor a translation, too much revised or emended, too much altered to count as a text of a given work. These are questions settled in practice by more or less arbitrary decision. Fortunately in the case of the great majority of works there is only a single text to consider, only a single candidate for family membership, so that we are not constantly called on to make such decisions. But any text is potentially the original ancestor of a family of texts, for any text can be translated and in various ways adapted. While there is good reason to distinguish work from text, it is necessary to recognize that the notion of a work is an incorrigibly vague one.

As we can speak of works, texts, and exemplars (performances and copies) in the case of writings, the written products of work, so we can distinguish, though we have fewer occasions to distinguish, those three elements in the case of human speech-acts, human talking. Most of our talk is, mercifully, unrecorded; but any of it might be recorded, in one way or another (for being *remembered* can be construed to count as being recorded), and any of it might then be considered as having a text, as having both an initial performance and a consequent copy or record of the performance, and as being a work of sorts. Only the most mindless mumblings cannot be considered as the doing of something, in addition to the producing of sounds and the producing of a text, the saying of one thing rather than another. It is always possible to characterize talk further, to describe what one is doing *in* saying what one is saying: exchanging pleasantries, lecturing, joking, sympathising, threatening, instructing, interrogating, and so on.[7] And so the text produced can be thought of as the text *of* the joke, the lecture, the threat, just as the text one writes out is taken as the text of a novel, a report, a letter. The threefold analysis of writings has its parallel in the case of sayings, the basic difference between the two sorts of cases being, perhaps, merely that one cannot write without producing a more or less permanent inscription, while only rarely does one's talk leave permanent physical traces.

We said above that the bibliographical universe was to consist of writings and recorded sayings. These are now to be understood as including inscriptions and performances of various sorts, as well as the texts of which these *are* inscriptions and performances, and the works of which the texts *are*

---

[7] See J. L. Austin, *How To Do Things With Words* (Oxford, 1962). What I am describing as things done are Austin's *illocutionary acts* (see pp. 98 et ff.). I make no use of what he calls "rhetic" acts, for I think I can do without them.

texts. Any inscription whatever is to be included, no matter what its form or its material vehicle; verbal or other performances will be included only if they leave a record behind or else are repeat performances of previously recorded texts. From a traditional standpoint our bibliographical universe may seem overcrowded; for it includes manuscripts as well as printed books, bills of lading and street signs as well as personal letters, inscriptions on stone as well as phonograph recordings of speeches, and most notably, memorized texts in human heads and texts stored up in the "memories" of machines.[8] But there is lexicographical warrant for taking "bibliography" to encompass manuscripts as well as printed books;[9] and is it not a comfortable move, from considering just printed books to considering books of all kinds, and thence to considering writings which are not "books" only because written on separate sheets that are not fastened together, or very brief, or never intended for general distribution?

If we recall that anything that is recorded in any form might also one day appear in printed form, and thus become an object of bibliographical concern in some narrow sense of "bibliography," we should wonder what virtue there can be in attending only to texts that at a given time happen to exist in printed form. The physical form in which a text happens to be embodied is inessential to its nature and interest, though not to its transmission and its availability. The printed book happened, for a while, to be the primary means of the exemplification of texts; but the problem of bibliographical control is not one arising simply from that physical form of exemplification of texts, for it might have existed had there been no printed books, and it would exist after printing was a forgotten art and books were found only in museums. But if it is true that the physical form in which texts are exemplified and so preserved does not determine the nature and interest of texts, then we are justified in including all of unwritten literature within the scope of bibliographical control; for a text remembered has, unless remembering is something purely spiritual, a physical representation, namely a condition or modification of the brain of the remember. A man's memory

---

[8] Except for the texts surviving only in memories, the items in our universe are the same as those frequently called "documents," for instance by Howard Mumford Jones in *One Great Society: Humane Learning in the United States* (New York 1959), p. 104: "... documents, by which we shall understand discourse, written, carved, or otherwise recorded.... Documents may be the latest novel, the text of a political treaty, the Rosetta stone, a Buddhist prayer, stenographic writing (as in the case of Pepys's diary), the morning newspaper (already become history), a cancelled check, and the like." Jones does not, but would, distinguish text and copy.

[9] See *Webster's New International Dictionary*, 2nd ed., *s.v. bibliography:* "the history or description of books and manuscripts...."

The Bibliographical Universe

of a text is an "object" of a very different sort from a book; but it is, for us, a perfectly good "bibliographical object."

Suppose that we could make an exhaustive inventory of the contents of the bibliographical universe. What should we want to count as one item in that universe? Obviously there is no single suitable way of choosing a counting unit. One natural way of starting would be by counting the distinct inscription-bearing physical objects, each distinct object to count as one item. So a librarian or bookseller might proceed, in taking stock, counting the separate volumes and loose issues of periodicals and loose manuscript leaves in his collection. But we might want, instead, to count each copy of a text as one item; and the number of text-bearing objects is by no means the same as the number of copies of texts. Any inscription-bearing object may contain copies of several texts, and a single copy of a text may occupy several volumes. If we are to count copies of texts, we must be able to tell one text from another, to say what counts as a single text, to say where, in a sequence of inscriptions, one text ends and another begins. Insofar as there is any "natural" way of doing this, one that depends neither on arbitrary decision or on convention, it is by reference to what the author considered to be one piece of work. Whether a sequence of words is a fragment of a larger text or is a complete text as it stands depends in large part, if not entirely, on whether the writer decides that it represents the completion of one job, or only the completion of one part of a job.

We may later assemble and disassemble texts in any ways we like; we may say that what the author calls one text has actually no "true unity," that it falls apart into pieces, and on such aesthetic grounds separate what the author had joined, or join what he separated. But if we imagine all a writer's manuscript pages piled together in random order, we must admit that not only does he have the final word on what page "really" follows what, but that he also has the final word on where one text stops and another starts; and this is, at least in large part, because each text represents to him the outcome of a distinct job or effort, a piece of work. Such appeal to the notion of a text as a piece of work is not always successful, and when it is not, convention or arbitrary decision must be appealed to. As there is a vagueness to the notion of a work, so there is a certain indefiniteness and arbitrariness about the notion of the size of the bibliographical universe, if that is made to depend on the number of copies of texts, or the number of texts of which there are copies; for what is one text is a question that frequently has no natural answer.

A complete inventory of the more or less enduring occupants of the bibliographical universe would be a list of all the copies of any text. From this basic inventory we could draw further inventories at will, of the texts represented by copies at a given time (as distinct from "lost" texts and from texts not yet composed), of the groups of objects containing copies of exactly the same texts, and so on.[10] Now though our inventory will not exclude copies that contain illustrations or diagrams or maps, we may well want to exclude maps, pieces of music, and pictures if the only bits of text they include are marginal notes or explanations or brief instructions. As it is hard to decide in general when a text is a text of a particular work, so it is hard to decide in general whether a picture or map illustrates a text, or whether a bit of text merely guides the interpretation of a map or picture.

There is, that is to say, no sharp boundary between the universe of writings and sayings, and the universe of pictorial and musical works. But there is good reason for distinguishing these universes, even though the distinction is not a sharp one. About any text we can ask "What does it mean, what language is it in, what is it about, what does it say?" and expect that, however hard it is to answer the questions, the questions surely do have answers. But though we may ask the same questions about a picture or a piece of music, it is not clear that they can be literally answered. Critics of art and music dispute over the possibility of ascribing "meaning" to works of art; but surely there is no doubt that, whether or not there is *some* sense in which they can have meaning, it is not the very same sense as that in which linguistic products have meaning.[11] A "language" without a dictionary or set of conventional assignments of senses to symbols, and without a syntax or way of combining symbols to allow of statements or

---

[10] One regrouping of items in the basic inventory would assemble all the copies of each edition in the textual sense of "edition," another would assemble all the copies of each edition in the (or one of the) physical sense of "edition." What I am calling the "physical sense" of the word is the sense in which an edition is a set of copies that have all been made by a single process, or by repeated application of the same process, and are thus closely if not exactly similar in appearance. It is in this sense that all the books printed from one setting up of type are said to comprise an edition, and in this sense that all the leaflets produced from a single set of mimeograph master sheets might be said to comprise an edition. In the "textual" sense, an edition is one of the texts of a work, and may appear in many different "physical" editions. A scholar's edition of *Hamlet* is a text, part of which is what he thinks is the best member of the *Hamlet*-family, the rest of which consists of his notes and commentary. On editions, see Fredson Bowers, *Principles of Bibliographical Description* (Princeton, 1949), chap. 2 and 11.

[11] See, for instance, John Hospers, *Meaning and Truth in the Arts* (Chapel Hill, N.C., 1946), or Monroe C. Beardsley, *Aesthetics* (New York, 1958).

The Bibliographical Universe 15

assertions, is not recognizably similar to the languages spoken by humans. An inventory of languages that included English, Chinese, and Sanskrit would not also include the "language of music" except as a joke. And while a man may claim that Rembrandt's portraits tell him profound things about humanity, and that Beethoven's late quartets have much to say about suffering, still it would be a curious performance to produce a bibliography in which were listed those pieces of music which were about suffering and about jealousy, and yet more curious to include brief abstracts of what they said about those things. A picture might be said, by extension, to be *about* what it is a picture *of*, and allegorical or symbolic pictures might be interpreted in a manner analogous to the way in which writings are interpreted; but there is only a remote analogy between the way in which a picture might be said to "tell" and the way in which we tell by talking. Many of the most important things to be said about writings have no, or only farfetched, analogues in the universe of pieces of music and pictures; and for this reason we shall not attempt to speak of that universe.[12]

Enough has been said to indicate the unsatisfactoriness of taking bibliographical control to be concerned exclusively with books. Let us now turn to the considerably more sophisticated notion that it should be construed as concerned with information. A universe of texts and copies and performances of texts may well strike some as composed of units of the wrong size and character. Those interested in texts for the factual information they contain, for the separate pieces or items of "knowledge" that may be found in them, are likely to find texts to be of inconvenient size and disconcerting heterogeneity. If one is looking for information on a specific point, one is as likely as not to be dismayed by the profusion of reports, journal articles, memoranda, treatises in which the information has to be sought. And such a one might say: We would do better to think of our task as that of defining control *directly* over units of information, rather than over the texts or copies of texts in which such units of information are to be found assembled and dispersed in a complicated way. The suggestion is not fanciful; people are found who will say that the job of li-

---

[12] What about maps? Do they not say something, at least "by implication"? Do we not "learn the language" of conventional signs and of contour intervals or layer tints? But the conventional signs are codes, not languages; there is no syntax supplied with the table of conventional signs. And apart from those signs, the map can be considered a picture, or the projection of a picture, which "means" and "says" things only in the extended and metaphorical sense in which a picture "means" and "says" things.

braries, or at least libraries of the future, is to furnish information rather than copies of texts, and one who says that about libraries can be easily imagined to say the same about bibliographical control.[18] If libraries come to be thought of as simply "storehouses of information," the bibliographical universe might come to be thought of simply as a universe of "recorded knowledge," and its primary units to be, not texts or copies of texts, but elementary facts or units of information. This would require a still greater change in the notion of "the bibliographical" than is required to see the bibliographical universe in the way proposed above; but no lexicographical or stylistic law prevents such change.

There is, or can easily be made to be, some plausibility in the suggestion. Much, though not all, of humanity's stock of knowledge is recorded in the texts of the bibliographical universe, and the relation of particular texts to the "body of knowledge" does indisputably figure largely in their evaluation, selection, and treatment in libraries and in bibliographies. If the physical medium in which a text is embodied is of only accidental interest, we might also claim that the textual environment or neighborhood in which an item of information or a bit of knowledge occurs is of only accidental interest. As we can analyze a single inscription-bearing physical object into as many "bibliographical objects" as there are copies of texts in or on the object, so we might think to analyze a single text into as many "informational objects" as there were distinguishable items of information contained in it. But while it is indisputable that texts can be analyzed much further than we have so far suggested, and equally indisputable that much of the value of texts derives from the information

---

[18] See Thomas Marill, *Libraries and Question-Answering Systems*, Report no. 1071, Bolt Beranek and Newman, Inc. (Cambridge, Mass. n. d.), leaves 6–7: "... the primary function of a library should be to provide, not documents, but information. ... The library of the future must be regarded not as a repository of documents with associated apparatus for document storage and retrieval, but rather as a central fund of organized information—that is to say, of knowledge—together with a body of techniques for up-dating this fund and for disseminating information in response to queries." See also J. C. R. Licklider, *Libraries of the Future* (Cambridge, Mass., 1965). And compare the extremely interesting work of J. Kaiser, *Systematic Indexing* (London, 1911), e.g., in this passage: "But for business purposes we must try to dissociate *information* from literature, we do not want books, we want information, and although this information is contained in books, it should be looked upon as quite a different material and it must be treated differently from books. Information taken away from literature can be organized more compactly, more homogeneously, and above all it gives us an opportunity to select better what we want, to reject what is of no use to us. As long as we have the information required we can get on quite well without any books at all" (para. 83). No doubt this is true for "business purposes," but even one serving those limited purposes must somehow discover the writings containing the information that will then be "taken away."

they contain, there are nevertheless many reasons for claiming that taking as unit the item of information rather than the text cannot be a *generally* advantageous procedure, however useful it might be in particular and limited circumstances. Let us consider a few of these reasons.

The first is the obvious fact, presumably not denied even by those most enthusiastic over the view of libraries and writings in general as containers of information, that most texts are not valued only for the information they contain, and that enormous numbers of them are not valued at all for their informational content. Of course the word "information" is presently used in such a great variety of ways that it would not be hard to find senses of "information" in which this obvious fact was not a fact at all. For example, the word "information" is sometimes used simply in the sense of "content," so that any meaningful statement (or almost any) would present information, and any paraphrase of a statement or any other formulation of what was meant or said or asserted by a statement would be a formulation of the informational content, i.e., the content, of the statement.[14] In this sense of "information," it is less clearly true that texts are valued for other reasons than the information they contain. But if we understand "information" in the more customary, and older, sense in which an item of information is a piece of fact, a factual claim about the world, presented as being true, then it is surely correct to say that texts are valued for other reasons than their informational content.[15] We do not, presumably, value *Religio Medici* and Law's *Serious Call* for their information, nor Plato's *Dialogues* nor Kant's *Critique of Pure Reason*. Gibbon and Thucydides relate many facts, but we do not read them solely to acquaint ourselves with those facts. Examples could be, but need not be, multiplied endlessly.

But even if a text were valued by someone solely because of its informativeness, it need not be valued by him solely because of the information it *contained,* but might rather be valued because of the information of which it was a *source*. A novel, for instance, in which there was no single literally true statement, might nevertheless be a valuable source of infor-

---

[14] This is roughly the sense the word bears in Rudolf Carnap and Y. Bar-Hillel, "An Outline of a Theory of Semantic Information," Technical Report no. 247 of the Research Laboratory of Electronics (Massachusetts Institute of Technology, 1952); reprinted in Bar-Hillel's *Language and Information* (Reading, Mass., 1964), pp. 221–274.

[15] "The word usually denotes a kind of knowledge that is gathered from other persons or from books and is accepted as truth; often, but not necessarily, with the implication that it has neither been confirmed nor verified . . ."—*Webster's Dictionary of Synonyms,* (Springfield, Mass., 1951), s.v. *knowledge.*

mation about the world; one might gather from it information of a sort that might in another place be explicitly asserted, might form the content of a text. What a text says is not necessarily what it reveals or what it allows us to conclude. Now if we think of a text as analyzed into its separate units of information, the only plausible course is to identify these with things said or asserted in a text, for we cannot directly recognize the things a text does not say but rather allows someone, under some circumstances, to conclude. The informational items into which a text might be resolved are items corresponding to claims made in the text, not to claims *not* made; but what is not said may interest us more than what is said.

In the sense in which we are now speaking of finding information in texts, what we are looking for are statements or assertions made in the text. Texts do not, of course, consist entirely of statements, and a text could not often be analysed without remainder into statements. "Who is Sylvia?" and "Go thou and do likewise" would not turn up in an inventory of items of information. Nor are all the declarative sentences we find statements or assertions. For instance, in the course of an argument one will frequently adopt an hypothesis one knows to be false in order to draw from it consequences that will show its falsity. To treat the presentation of the hypothesis as a statement of the hypothesis, that is, an assertion of the hypothesis, would be a blunder. But then the assertions we do find are by no means independent of their environment or context; unless they are extensively rewritten, their proper interpretation may be undiscoverable when they are examined in isolation. A unit of information or knowledge could not, in general, be identified with a particular string of words in a text, but would have to be identified with some translation or reformulation of strings of words in such a way as to be correctly interpretable outside any context.[16] But this is precisely what cannot be done completely, except for the most banal sort of statement. A particular statement in a text can frequently be understood only in terms of most or all of its surrounding

---

[16] The translation or reformulation would approximate to what Quine calls "eternal sentences," W. V. O. Quine, *Word and Object* (New York, 1960), pp. 193 ff. et passim. Strictly speaking a unit of information could never under any circumstances be identified with a string of words or a sentence, but rather with the content of a sentence, the "proposition" expressed by the sentence. A further good reason for eschewing analysis of texts into units of information is just this fact, that units of information would have to be identified with abstract entities of a particularly obscure sort. The relation of text to its copies is not essentially an obscure one, I think; the relation of a proposition to what expresses that proposition is exceedingly obscure.

text, and if taken as a separate unit of "information" could not be made intelligible short of rewriting so as to include the whole text from which it was initially detached. But if a text does not ordinarily consist of declarative sentences only, if declarative sentences cannot be regularly identified with statements or assertions, if assertions can be understood only in terms of their surrounding context, the notion of analyzing a text into detachable separate items of information loses any plausibility.

Finally, not only the understanding of a statement but the *appraisal* of a statement depends on seeing it in its original habitat. Claims or statements are true or false, well or ill supported, more or less credible or trustworthy. And when one seeks information in texts, one does not look simply for factual assertions, but for believable ones. One wants correct information, wants to be informed rather than misinformed, wants knowledge rather than error. But how can one judge the credibility or trustworthiness of a claim except by seeing who said it and how he supported it? A mere collection of assertions is of no interest to the seeker for information, unless he has some way of deciding which members of the collection can be taken to be true or well supported. Texts form, as it were, the basic contexts in which individual assertions have sense and from which their credibility can be assessed.

For all these reasons, and more that might be adduced, it will not be advantageous to make our account of bibliographical control apply generally to units smaller than whole texts and copies of them. This does not mean that we are interested only in whole texts. Much of the ensuing discussion will concern identification and description of parts or ingredients of texts. Nor is this meant to question the obvious utility of assembling all "known facts" about some range of phenomena into handbooks or compendia of "data." It is, however, to deny that writings can be adequately viewed as consisting of discrete items of the sort appropriate for handbooks of "data." The problem of bibliographical control is not simply one of locating items of information, and not one to be solved by attempting to analyze writings into units of information.

Chapter II

DESCRIBING AND EXPLOITING

We have only begun to describe a power when we have said what it is power over; we must go on to describe the things that one who has that power can do or have done. What might a person be able to do or have done to things in the bibliographical universe that would count as exercises of the power we call "bibliographical control"? There seem to me to be two quite distinct sorts of things that deserve to be called exercises of bibliographical control. Of these two, one is the more familiar, but the other is the more important. Let us approach the latter first.

Much, but happily not all, of the reading we do is purposive: we read in order to find an answer to a particular question, to learn what is known of some range of phenomena, to improve our understanding of some matter, to find out how to do a certain sort of thing, to maintain or improve our social or intellectual position, to console ourselves in our misfortunes. If asked why we want to do these things, we are often able to cite a further goal: we want to find out how to make a chocolate mousse because we want to serve one to our dinner guests, we want to find out how much weight a given sort of rope will support because we want to hang ourselves. And the further goal mentioned might itself be explained in terms of a still further goal. Sometimes we cite no further goal; we claim simply to be curious, which is a way of saying that there is no further goal behind our immediate goal. But whenever we read for a purpose, whether or not there is a further purpose behind our immediate purpose, we may happen to read what is not the best, or not a very good, thing to read in order to attain our immediate goal: it may give misinformation, it may be too technical or not technical enough, it may be superficial or too deep, it may omit what would be most important for us and be full of what is of no importance. That we do not have what would be best for our purpose may not be entirely regrettable, if what we have is intrinsically interesting to us, or if it later turns out that our having had that purpose at that time was itself regrettable or mistaken. But if we really do have a purpose in reading, we cannot be indifferent to the quality of what we read, considered as an instrument for the attainment of that purpose; we must care whether what we have is as good as could be had, whether we have the most suitable instrument. We may of course not care very much about the quality of the instrument, but then it must also be true that we do not care very much about attaining our goal. Indifference to the quality of the instrument chosen for use in pursuit of a goal, which one claimed to think of great importance, would indicate a curious, an almost unintelligible irrationality of conduct; a man may not reflect much or carefully on the suitability of the means he chooses to attain a goal, but he cannot without irrationality be quite indifferent to the quality of the means.[1]

We may say then that in those cases in which a person thinks he can attain, or get some way towards attaining, a goal by means of reading, he would like to be able to have the best means available for the attainment of that goal, to have what we can call the *best textual means* to his end.[2] That a person rejected what he himself admitted to be the best writing for his purpose in favor of what he himself admitted to be inferior would be an indication of madness, or would at the least require a good deal of explanation. It would not be irrational for a man to refrain from making any effort to procure a better means than was immediately available to him, if what he had would in his opinion serve well enough, would be at least minimally adequate; but if no effort at all were required to procure the best, deliberate choice of the worse would be unintelligible. It is a necessary truth, not about human conduct in general but about

---

[1] The bureaucrat without control over the flow of papers to his desk may find such talk wryly amusing; for his reading is purposive, but the notion of means to an end seems inapplicable in his case. Indeed it is, if he must read whatever comes his way, for then he has no choice, and so no concern about the best choice. But if he can choose to read some and not others, or if he has some control over the content or style of what comes his way, then what is said applies to his case. Other cases in which freedom of choice is absent will come to mind: the proofreader, the student assigned a text. Where there is no choice to be made among different texts, there is no such thing as power of the first sort.

[2] Notions akin to this one turn up here and there in writings on information retrieval. For instance, Goffman and Newill write: "Since the query which the user has posed to the system [an information retrieval system] is a formal representation of some user need, it follows [sic] that documents that are relevant to the query may not necessarily be appropriate to the user's need. A subset of the file [of documents in the system] which is appropriate to the need is called a *pertinent set,* and the property which assigns members to this set is called pertinence."—William Goffman and Vaun A. Newill, *Methodology for Test and Evaluation of Information Retrieval Systems,* Technical report no. 2, Comparative Systems Laboratory, Center for Documentation and Communication Research, School of Library Science, Western Reserve University (Cleveland, 1964), leaf 7. I suppose they mean that pertinence is appropriateness to a need; the most pertinent would be the most appropriate and, on a suitable understanding of "appropriate," would thus be the best textual means available in the file for the satisfaction of the need. For reasons discussed in Chapter IX below, I prefer to avoid talk of needs.

rational conduct, that one will always prefer to have what one believes to be the best means available for the attainment of one's goals. Like other necessary truths, this one is also almost trivially true, and apparent counter-examples will always be accommodated by suitable qualifications.[3] But though we learn nothing new by reflecting on such almost empty truths, still we may remind ourselves thereby of one general goal that is present in all instances of rational purposive use of writings: one would like the best textual means to one's ends. To be able always to procure the best means would be, I claim, to have the highest degree of the more important of two sorts of bibliographical control. The briefest satisfactory way of describing what it would be like to have the more important sort of bibliographical control is this: to have the power to procure the best textual means to one's ends.

Before beginning the necessary elaboration and qualification of this brief account, let us turn to the second, no doubt more readily recognizable, sort of bibliographical control. For many reasons, or for no reason at all, a person might want produced or identified for him all the writings fitting a certain description: all those written by Hobbes, all those discussing the doctrine of eternal recurrence, all those containing the word "fatuity"; and if he were able to have the writings fitting his description produced or identified, he would clearly have a sort of power, *a* bibliographical power if not *the* bibliographical power. But exactly how does this sort of power differ from the first? The examples just given are examples of descriptions that are, we shall say, *evaluatively neutral,* and it is this "neutrality" that is meant to distinguish exercises of the second from exercises of the first sort of power. An exercise of the first sort of power essentially involves the *appraisal* of writings (though not necessarily appraisal by him who has the power), the estimation of the merits and defects of writings in terms of credibility, of intelligibility, of accuracy, of adaptability or utility, of scholarship, and so on through the catalogue of virtues and vices. It also requires appraisal of appropriateness or suitability to a particular individual's situation, depending thus on estimates of his knowledge, his capacities, the intensity of his interest in his goal, the energy he has available and the amount of it he is willing to spend, the time at his disposal and the amount of it he is willing to

---

[3] If, for instance, cases are cited of preference for the worse over the better because of some undesirable side effects of use of the best, it is simply pointed out that "best" means "best on the whole, that is, taking into consideration all side effects."

give up, how far along he is already towards achieving his goal, and so on. In contrast to this, power of the second sort requires no appraisals of value or utility or suitability on anyone's part;[4] it is a power to have called up arbitrary classes of writings, described in terms involving no element of appraisal and requiring no evaluations of writings in order to decide whether or not they fit the description presented. One who was always able to have supplied all the writings or an arbitrary selection of writings satisfying some evaluatively neutral description would have the highest degree of this sort of power.

This second sort of power seems incontestably to include the powers most frequently discussed under the label of "bibliographical control." But by making it include the ability to have supplied writings satisfying *any* arbitrarily chosen description, so long as the description is a "neutral" one, do we not make an unjustified extension of the notion of bibliographical control? It might be said: there are "bibliographical" properties of writings, and "non-bibliographical" properties, and only questions or demands specified in terms of the former are properly bibliographical questions or bibliographical demands, properly defining the scope of bibliographical control. Not every fact about a writing is a bibliographical fact, and not until the line between bibliographical and non-bibliographical facts is clearly *and correctly* drawn can we have a proper idea of the nature of bibliographical control.

But as we saw no sufficient reason to limit membership in the bibliographical universe to some subset of the set of writings and recorded sayings, so we shall, I think, find no sufficient reason to exclude some sorts of questions about those writings and recorded sayings as "not properly bibliographical questions." We might draw a line between bibliographical and non-bibliographical properties of writings (or, more properly, of copies) where the historical bibliographer draws it, but since, in his sense of "bibliography," "bibliography has nothing whatever to do with the subject or literary content of the book,"[5] the result would be that no ques-

---
[4] This claim must be taken cautiously; to decide whether a given writing fits a neutral description may require appraisal of something other than that writing, for instance, evidence supporting the statement that its author is so-and-so. But such cases do not require appraisal of the writing itself, and if they did, would not fall into our second category. I ignore the complications presented by the possibility that attributions of authorship are sometimes made on the basis of evaluations, that people will say a writing cannot be by so-and-so because it is so poor.

[5] W. W. Greg, "Bibliography—A Retrospect," in *The Bibliographical Society, 1892–1942: Studies in Retrospect* (London, 1945), p. 24.

tion framed in terms of the content of writings would be a bibliographical question. But no one wants to say that bibliographical control has nothing whatever to do with the subject or literary content of writings, and so this way of distinguishing bibliographical from non-bibliographical properties is necessarily unsatisfactory.

On the other hand, we might try to make the distinction by referring to what bibliographers, that is, makers of lists, know how to do, or by referring to what bibliographers do in fact do. If we try the former of these two ways, again the result will be unsatisfactory; for it is not in virtue of his knowledge of how to make lists that a bibliographer identifies authors and subjects of writings, and so questions about authorship or subject matter would not be questions that could be posed in an exercise of bibliographical control, which is absurd. But if we try the second of these two ways, the distinction cannot be made at all. For *any* sort of fact about a writing might be recorded in a bibliography. We do not make a list of writings, described very minutely, into a bibliography by *omitting* all except some tiny set of descriptive details; there are perhaps some sorts of information a list *must* contain if it is to be called a bibliography, but none that it must *not* contain. So we cannot distinguish bibliographical from non-bibliographical facts about writings by referring to what can, and what cannot, be recorded in a bibliography.

We might, finally, try to make the distinction in terms of what can be discovered about writings (texts or copies) by simple inspection, by merely looking or reading without further study. But what is the virtue of making bibliographical control so very superficial a matter? It would be easier to achieve if it concerned only what was evident to the stupidest bibliographer, but it would scarcely be worth achieving. The stupidest bibliographer might be able to recognize a personal name on a title page, but the authorship of a writing is not something that can be determined by simple inspection of the writing, so a distinction based on degree of superficiality is as unsatisfactory as the others.

Let us say, then, that bibliographical questions are, simply, questions about writings; there is no need for a distinction between bibliographical and non-bibliographical properties of writings, and no need to limit the variety of descriptions that can enter into questions posed in exercises of bibliographical control.[6] Most of the possible questions are not answer-

---

[6] But of course anyone else may limit the notion as he pleases; I argue only that there is no conclusive reason for limiting the notion, not that the notion cannot be limited.

able, because no one knows all there is to know about any set of writings; but we need set no limit in advance to the extent of knowledge of bibliographical facts, facts about texts or writings.

The two sorts of power now roughly described might be contrasted as "exploitative control" and "descriptive control." "Exploitative control" is a deliberately somewhat rough or severe term for the ability to make the best use of a body of writings, "descriptive control" a not very adequate term for an ability to line up a population of writings in any arbitrary order, to make the population march to one's command. The wielder of perfect descriptive control can have summoned up every writing[7] that fits his arbitrary description, so long as the applicability of the description to particular writings can be discovered without any consideration of virtues or vices or utilities; the wielder of perfect exploitative control has merely to say what he wants writings *for*, and is then provided with what will suit that purpose best, whatever it is. Now it is hard to see why a person who had exploitative control over a body of writings should care about having descriptive control; for what are the occasions on which, given that one could procure immediately the best textual means to one's ends, one would want to have the whole population sorted out according to some principle of division that made no mention of fitness for any purpose or end? The primary purpose in calling for all items of some sort is, one would think, to choose from them the best, or most suitable, for some purpose or other, or simply to appraise them; but if we could have that done for us, what motive would remain, except caprice or idle curiosity, for wanting all, or a random selection, of any neutrally described class of writings? Of course idle curiosity knows no bounds, and being able to satisfy caprice and idle curiosity is a precious power; but surely it is a power of lower value than the power to have supplied the best means to one's ends.

Let us put this in another way. The rationale for desiring exploitative control is obvious; in saying what it is, one also shows why one should want it, or can show this merely by reference to the necessary truth about rational behavior set out earlier. But the rationale for desiring descriptive control is far from obvious. I suggest that, apart from the desire to be able to indulge one's whims and idle curiosity, the only reason for desiring that power is as a substitute for the other, greater, but less easily

---

[7] "Every writing" in the field under his control, every writing without exception only if that field is the whole bibliographical universe.

obtainable power. The only reason for wanting the ability to line up a population in arbitrary ways is that one lacks the other power, and has oneself to attempt discovery of the best textual means to one's ends by scrutiny of members of various neutrally described classes of the population. It may be that the greater power will never be fully available to anyone, that we shall always have to make do with the inferior substitute; but that does nothing to show that descriptive control is not an inferior substitute.

It will be argued that the inferior power is still necessary, as a precondition of the possession of the superior power, that I cannot have supplied the best textual means unless it is known (to someone, at some time) what are all the available means, and therefore unless there is descriptive control (possessed by someone, at some time). Now the sense in which descriptive control can be claimed to be a precondition of exploitative control is not at all obvious; one does not, to take a simple example, discover the best introduction to a given subject simply by examining the set of writings described as "introductions" to that subject. We shall return later to the question of the exact sense in which one sort of power is a precondition of the other. But I think that we can claim that, whatever that sense may be, it does nothing to show that descriptive control is the more valuable. At best it would show that we cannot have the more valuable unless we also have the less valuable. This is hardly surprising, if true; that we cannot have knowledge without hard study does not show knowledge less valuable than hard study, and if we were able, by a miracle, to have the one without the other, most of us would gladly take the knowledge and let the study go. So it is with bibliographical control.

Can there be any doubt at all that people would indeed like to have exploitative control? It is customary to say that one of the greatest problems of reference librarians and operators of "information systems" is to discover what a patron's request "really" is, to discover what it is he "really" wants. I do not know how seriously the attempt to discover "real" desires is made; but I think it almost beyond reasonable doubt that sufficient exploration would discover that what appear to be questions of the descriptive sort would almost invariably turn out to be questions of the exploitative sort, or that almost any "real" desire would be expressible only in appraisive terms. In practically every demand anyone makes on the bibliographical apparatus he employs, what he wants, whether he announces the fact or not, is what will be good for, or the best for, doing something he wants to do. At times, certainly, the question of what is best need not arise, for anything fitting a certain neutral description will do. Anything may serve as a temporary doorstop, and a man who demanded the best doorstop, when all he needed was something to hold a door open for a moment or two, would be though preposterous. And so there are occasions on which what we want to do with texts might be done equally well by anything satisfying some quite neutral description.

We can imagine a person who wanted merely some, no matter which, nineteenth-century tract on the Corn Laws—though the request for "any, no matter which" is most likely to conceal an actual desire for a representative tract, one which is a good or fair example, not in truth any arbitrarily chosen one. A person might ask for "a current text book in economics, any one will do," a request which again probably conceals a desire for a decently representative work, not a cranky, heretical, or terribly reactionary text. In most cases the desire for something good for one's purposes is lambently clear; if I ask for discussions of the Pelagian heresy or an analysis of Aristotle's *Metaphysics,* it is practically certain that I want a good discussion or analysis, not one that is confused, historically inaccurate, unscholarly, and in an unreadable style. If I want to know about some point of physiology which I suppose to be discussed in every standard treatise on physiology, and if I ask for "any physiological treatise," have I not really misstated my desire? For I want the truth, or a work containing the truth. Since there is no mark by which we humans can recognize the truth when we see it,[8] we have invariably to make do with the best opinion we can get, the best attested opinion. I do not in fact want just any physiological treatise, but one which is as trustworthy as any, one whose discussion of

---

[8] This is dogmatically said; to "prove" it would take volumes. William James puts the problem nicely: "But the faith that truth exists, and that our minds can find it, may be held in two ways. We may talk of the *empiricist* way and of the *absolutist* way of believing in truth. The absolutists in this matter say that we not only can attain to knowing truth, but we can *know when* we have attained to knowing it: while the empiricists think that although we may attain it, we cannot infallibly know when. To *know* is one thing, and to know for certain *that* we know is another. One may hold to the first being possible without the second . . ."—*The Will to Believe* (New York, 1956), p. 12. I am denying the "absolutist" way; for a defense of absolutism one might consult Cardinal Mercier, *A Manual of Modern Scholastic Philosophy* (various editions), sections on Criteriology, or Mercier's *Critériologie générale* (various editions). It might be salutary if those who talk of stores of information and knowledge would force themselves to speak instead of stores of what we think at present, on better or worse evidence, to be true. To talk of knowledge or information has a satisfactorily objective, impersonal air. But our actual position is that various conflicting claims are made to us, and when we accept some as "knowledge" and reject others as "falsehood," we are doing our characteristic human job of evaluating conflicting claims.

the point that interests me will be credible, worthy of belief, and I would seriously want any arbitrary treatise only if I thought (what cannot be correct) that on my point they are equally trustworthy.

Let us take it as obvious enough that when I ask for information, I do really want information, and not misinformation; any such request requires evaluation of writings in terms of their credibility. If I ask for an explanation of something, I want a writing that does explain, that gives a correct account, as well as a lucid account; any such request involves evaluation of writings, in terms of credibility and lucidity. There are other sorts of evaluations, too many to be listed. I might want a good collection of examples of some phenomenon: good written exemplifications, for instance, of the psychological mechanisms of adjustment of handicapped persons, good examples of scientific "fallacies" among autodidacts. Judging the suitability or excellence of a writing as an example of some phenomenon is a distinct sort of evaluation. Again, I might want writings that provided the best evidence for or against an hypothesis: not merely those which have been mistakenly supposed to provide evidence, but those that do. But to describe a writing as providing evidence for or against an hypothesis is to appraise it, in a particularly complex fashion.

Again, I might want writings that would best serve as sources from which I could reconstruct a patch of history, and if I cannot in fact trust others to distinguish the genuine from the spurious and the important from the insignificant, I still admit the desirability of that service. But identifying a document as important is obviously another sort of evaluation. Again, I might, as a technician or technologist, want writings containing discoveries or results of pure scientific investigation that have useful applications in my work; but no more complicated appraisal can well be imagined than that which judges the utility of a piece of scientific work in practical application.[9] Again, for one reason or another I might want rhetorically powerful or stylistically elegant writings on some topic or directed to some given end, writings that will put a case as well as it can be put, or influence those one wishes to persuade, if they can be influenced

---

[9] "It must not be supposed that the connexion between basic research and its final industrial application is a simple one.... One cannot match each piece of basic research with its applications, for a great part of scientific knowledge has no industrial application so far perceived. The ideas now being applied may have had their beginning a long time ago. Thus the new electronics industry depends ultimately on basic research on electrons started by J. J. Thomson and others at the end of the last century. In the early 1930's Lord Rutherford foresaw no practical application of his atom-splitting experiments..."—C. F. Carter and B. R. Williams, *Industry and Technical Progress* (London, 1957), p. 19.

at all. Rhetorical and stylistic value represent appraisals that would have to be made to satisfy some of my requests. The variety of appraisals necessary to satisfy all my requests would be enormous; but appraisal, in one or another guise, would be required to satisfy almost all of them. And the possession of descriptive control alone would allow almost none of those requests to be satisfied directly.

The two sorts of power have been contrasted as sharply as possible, as is desirable in an exercise in analysis. No doubt the limited powers actually possessed by people are complex mixtures of the two. But it might be claimed that the two sorts of power are really only one, that there is no *essential* difference between them; and the reason given might be that, if we were to imagine what it would be like to have either sort of power in the highest degree, we can do so only by means of a thought-experiment in which the difference between the two becomes negligible, as trivial as would be a division of descriptive control itself into a thousand different sorts of power, a different power for every different sort of feature of writings we might mention.

In discussions of information storage and retrieval there is frequently presented an ideal of performance which suggests the "unity" of the two types of bibliographical control. An ideal system of information storage and retrieval is customarily described as one in which, in response to a question or demand, there was produced all and only the relevant information, or all and only the relevant documents, or information or documents relevant to some specified degree, to the question posed or the demand made. Against this standard of perfection the actual performance of systems is to be measured. Unless "relevance" is explained, we have no idea of what this ideal performance would be like, and we shall presently investigate that word pretty fully.

But there is one way in which it has been suggested we should understand the ideal performance of a system, which gives content to the notion of relevance. That way is to imagine what a person would himself select were he to read through the entire contents of all the writings contained in a system.[10] Suppose a person is seeking the best textual means to some end,

---

[10] See Don R. Swanson, "The Formulation of the Retrieval Problem," in Paul Garvin, ed., *Natural Language and the Computer* (New York, 1963), p. 255: "...this viewpoint [i.e., imagining what a person would select were he to read through an entire collection of documents] is useful and thought provoking, since it is by no means obvious that there exists any *other* way to attain what we may define as 'perfect' retrieval."

or all writings fitting some neutral description: then what he would like is the power to have provided for him just those texts which he would select himself, were he to read through the entire corpus of writings subject to his control. The set of writings he would himself select becomes the ideal set,[11] defining perfect control in respect of a single question or demand, and always to be provided with the ideal set for any possible question would be to have perfect bibliographical control. But then we can unify our two sorts of control; the nature of a power is given by citing the nature of the results of exercise of the power, and if all exercises of either sort of power result in getting what one would have selected oneself, then there is basically just one sort of power.

The thought-experiment of reading through corpora of writings cannot, however, possibly provide a satisfactory account of ideal performance of information systems or of perfect bibliographical control. If I do indeed want the best textual means to a given end, then in the ideal situation I am given that, but I shall certainly not suppose that I could always or usually recognize it if I stumbled across it. If I want evidence for a theory, then that is what I want, not what I might suppose to be evidence; and I shall not claim that I can always recognize what is evidence on first looking at it. If I want what will help me understand some phenomenon, then that is what I want, even if it is not seen to be of help for a long time; but I do not claim the ability to see that a writing is going, after prolonged study, to produce illumination. It is true that I might be given what excellent authority assured me would be of help to me, or was the best for my purpose, or provided strong evidence for my hypothesis; and I might still after much study be unable to see that the claim was justified. One possible reaction in such a case would be to deny that the claim was justified; but another would be to say: the claim may be justified, but I am unable to see how. The times one most needs help, which one might hope to get from a "retrieval system" that was as good as possible, are the times when one would *not* be able to pick out the items that would help. And that one did not see that what was offered as helpful was indeed so, would not neces-

---

[11] Goffman and Newill (op. cit., leaf 7): "... a uniquely defined subset of the file which serves as a basis for measuring variation in systems performance. This set is called the *ideal set*, and in the initial phases of experiments the ideal set will be represented by that subset of the file the user would have selected as a response to his query had he searched the file himself.. This set shall also be referred to as the *relevant* set."

sarily falsify the claim that one had been given what was best for one.[12]

Again, it is obvious that if I ask for a complete set of the extant writings of Plato, then perfect control, or perfect performance of my "retrieval system," would consist in my being given a complete set, and just that. But this does not bear at all on the question whether I can tell by examining a writing that it is by Plato; to get what is by Plato, and to get what I think may be by Plato, are in principle very different things, and I would prefer the former ability to the latter.

We may, I think, go this far: perfect performance, whether of an "information retrieval system" or of arrangements for bibliographical control, can *never* be defined or even adequately illustrated by reference to what one would select were he to examine entire corpora of writings.[13] The consequence may be drawn that if a perfectly working information system existed, we would not be able to recognize it, and if we had perfect bibliographical control, we could not distinguish it from various imperfect situations. This is, I think, perfectly true, and not on reflection a bit surprising. There may be somewhere a man who constantly makes predictions about the remote future, and retrodictions about the remote past, all of which are in fact correct. We could not recognize such a man; but this inability is not surprising, and does not reflect at all on the intelligibility of the description of him just given. When we define an ideal condition, we may very well recognize that it is one whose actual existence we could never detect.

So we have not been forced, by the thought experiment imagined, to abandon our claim that there are two distinct sorts of bibliographical power or control. But we have repulsed only the lightest assault. It could still be

---
[12] Rees mentions some further reasons for rejecting this account of ideal performance of an information retrieval system. "Unfortunately, the customer will select a different set today than he would tomorrow; if he were in Fargo, North Dakota instead of Washington, D. C., his selection might very well be different; if he examined each document in a different sequence his assessment of relevance would not be the same [and so his selection would differ]."—Alan M. Rees, *The Evaluation of Retrieval Systems,* Technical report no. 5, Comparative Systems Laboratory, Center for Documentation and Communication Research, School of Library Science, Western Reserve University (Cleveland, 1965), leaf 4.

[13] I do not mean that there are no cases in which people would themselves be able to identify the items they request, but that we cannot explain what we *mean* by perfect performance by referring to what people happen to do. And cases in which people would be able to identify the items they requested are not adequate illustrations of perfect performance, because they do not clearly exhibit the difference between, for instance, getting the best and getting the worst textual means. An adequate illustration is one that clearly exhibits, points up, singles out, the feature one is trying to illustrate.

argued that, at a "deeper" level, the distinction might disappear, either because requests framed in terms of suitability of means to ends could always be replaced by, if not "reduced" to, requests framed in terms of some combination of neutral descriptions, or because there is no difference of kind, but only a difference in degree along a single scale between neutral descriptions and appraisals or evaluations.

On the first line of argument, it would be claimed that as a person who wants the best automobile or refrigerator for his purposes can specify the tests which would establish that one automobile or refrigerator was better than another for his purposes, tests which could be conducted by the most severely neutral investigator, tests which did not require evaluation but merely counting and measuring and such "objective" operations, so too it would be possible always to replace a request for the best textual means by a specification of the "objective criteria" by which value would be determined. If this were true then, whether or not it meant the same thing to ask for the best means to an end, and to ask for items satisfying some complex description couched in non-evaluative terms, there would be a factual equivalence between the two sorts of requests and the residual difference in meaning could be forgotten.

On the second line of argument, it would be claimed that insofar as we can distinguish between evaluating and ("neutrally") describing, some element of each enters into every remark we ever make about anything, that there are no pure cases of evaluation and none of description, but at best a continuum extending indefinitely in both directions, the end points being unreachable. But if we never make a purely evaluative remark, and never make a purely descriptive remark, what becomes of the difference in kind between requests for what must be evaluated and requests for what need only be described?

The two arguments, if pursued, would carry us directly to the heart of the philosophical study of value, a study in which analogous arguments have successfully resisted dissolution for centuries.[14] We can hardly do more than bow in the direction of that study, and then continue as if it did not exist. For we do know, what would not be denied by any student of

---

[14] The following works might be recommended to those unfamiliar with modern Anglo-American writings on value-theory and connected subjects: J. O. Urmson, "On Grading," in *Logic and Language,* 2nd Ser., ed. Antony Flew (Oxford, 1955), pp. 159–186; R. M. Hare, *The Language of Morals* (Oxford, 1952); P. H. Nowell-Smith, *Ethics* (Harmondsworth, Penguin Books, 1954); Philippa Foot, "Goodness and Choice," *Aristotelian Society Supplementary Volume,* 35 (1961), pp. 45–60.

value-theory, that whatever might be true in theory, in fact we are not, always or ever, able to give exact accounts of the "objective criteria" by which the suitability of texts to our purposes could be determined. And if pure cases of evaluation or description are hard to find or even non-existent, still there is that practical difference between requests requiring so little evaluation that even a machine could answer them, and requests requiring so much that only a person of nice judgment can be entrusted with them. So we shall maintain our commonsense distinction between powers whose exercise requires appraisal and those whose exercise requires only bare description, between those involving the ability to see what writings are good for and those involving only the ability to see what they are.

Mention of "objective criteria" of evaluation provides a suitable occasion for the following general observation about attempts to anticipate the future utilities of writings. Even if it were true that we could, for each individual case as it was presented, state the "objective criteria" in terms of which the best textual means could be identified, we could not possibly anticipate, at any given time, either all the varieties of individual cases that might in future arise, or all the features of writings that might on occasion be among the "objective criteria" of value. As there is no limit to the number and variety of purposes that people may entertain, so also we cannot exhaustively list the characteristics on which the utility of a writing may sometime depend. There is an obvious corollary to this. If we were to formulate a single measure of value of individual writings, a measure that would assign a unique value to each item on the basis of a set of "objective criteria" however complex, it is clear in advance that such a measure must be inadequate in an indefinitely large number of cases. However we chose to rank or score or evaluate writings, our method would fail to reflect the suitability of writings to some possible purposes and for some possible individual situations. Further, no collection of different measures of value that we could formulate would be sufficient. But a further corollary is this: as we cannot evaluate writings now in such a way as to meet all future cases, we cannot describe writings in sufficient detail to allow future evaluation on the basis of our descriptions alone, for we cannot know what characteristics of writings will be of decisive importance in future situations. Neither evaluation nor description could be done once and for all, that is, done so adequately that no future re-evaluation or re-description would be needed for perfectly adequate selection of best textual means to given ends. This is not to say it is pointless to try to improve our methods of providing for future needs; but it is to say that we cannot, in principle, expect that any provision we made at one time would be completely satisfactory at later times. The significance of these general claims, if not now clear, will become so in our later discussions of the bibliographical apparatus.

There is a last objection to our claims about two sorts of power that I wish to consider, one which will lead us to a certain refinement of our account. It may be claimed that there are other sorts of power over texts than the two we have distinguished, that our two sorts are, if indeed distinct, still not exhaustive of the whole range of bibliographical powers. First, the ability to acquire a copy, or command a performance, of any individual text one liked and could uniquely describe might seem a distinct sort of power. Is asking for and getting a copy of *Trent's Last Case* an exercise of exploitative control, or descriptive? The answer is that it might be either. If I wanted to read that work, I would not want just any copy, but a suitable one: portable, legible, attractive. And my purpose would be to read *Trent's Last Case,* but that work is a family of many members, and the different texts would not be equally suitable (a Norwegian translation would hardly do me much good). I would be indifferent neither to choice of text nor to choice of copy, and if the notion of *best* means seems otiose, that is simply because so many different copies would do equally well. If I wanted to do nothing at all with the work, but idly asked for a random copy of the work, my getting one could perfectly well be taken as an instance of descriptive control. In such a case, that aspect or dimension of power we shall call "supply" is the most important. Let us put aside discussion of that aspect for a moment and consider a more serious sort of case. Suppose a person wants the best books on, say, the history of Crete: he has no purpose in mind, is engaged in no inquiry, does not even want to read anything on Crete, has just whimsically decided to fill his bookshelves with the best, but only the best, books on Crete. Can we imagine his getting them? And if we can, must we not say this is a distinct sort of power? For exploitative control is described in terms of means to ends, and descriptive control in terms of appraisal-free descriptions of writings.

To answer this question, let us re-examine the notion of exploitative control. That was explained as the power to have supplied the best textual means to one's ends; I would have that power to the extent that my requirements could be met, you would have it to the extent that your requirements could be met. Now nothing requires us to consider only actual requirements; my power would be in part measured by my ability to have a certain sort of requirement met, even if I never in fact made that requirement, never in fact set myself the aim for which I could have the best textual means. So an individual's power is determined not merely by what he can get when he does want textual means to ends, but by what he could get if and when he *did* want textual means to various ends. This is the first step in our argument. Next, though what is best for me may not, and very frequently will not, be what is best for you, nevertheless I might want, out of benevolence or greed, to be able to procure for you what would be the best means to your various ends. You might conceivably lack the power to procure the best textual means, but I might be able to do it for you. Now if I could do this for everyone, my power would be in a certain dimension *universal*. It is just this universality of power at which every good reference librarian aims, though none attains it. The reference librarian with this sort of power could procure for any one the best textual means to the attainment of any end.

Now we can deal sufficiently well with the man who wants the best books on Cretan history. What could he conceivably be after? We might take a request for the best books on Cretan history to be a request for those books that are most highly regarded by, say, "the experts" on Cretan history. If that is the request, it can be filled without any evaluation, for to report the popularity or standing of a writing among a certain class of men is not itself to evaluate the writing at all. Suppose this is not what is meant. Then the value of a writing must be judged in terms of its capability of serving various human interests and concerns, that is, in terms of its suitability as a means to the attainment of various possible ends. Whatever features of a writing that one took to be merits and defects would be features that would determine the suitability of a writing as means to some ends, and the ability to get the "best books" on Cretan history, if not the same as the power to get best textual means to one's own ends, would not be different from some degree of the power to provide others with textual means to their ends.[15] No new power seems to be represented by our imagined case, then, but simply either an exercise of descriptive control, or an exercise of exploitative control where the ends served are not one's own but others'.

We have complicated our account of exploitative control by introducing a "dimension" corresponding to the number of other individuals for whom

---

[15] This may not satisfy those who believe in an "intrinsic goodness" inexplicable in terms of human purposes and priorities; such believers may want to define a third sort of bibliographical power.

a given individual can procure best textual means; the greatest degree of power in this dimension would be represented by the ability to serve the whole world. There are a number of other dimensions that must also be distinguished, a number of distinct ways in which a power may vary in the directions of increase and decrease. Power, like ability, must be described in terms that allow for occasional failures and breakdowns; a man may fail to do on a given occasion what he is still correctly said to be able to do, and likewise may have the power to command what on a given occasion does not occur at command. Still, in estimating the amount of bibliographical control that a man has, it is necessary to consider how regularly, and how well, his demands are fulfilled. This we can call the dimension of reliability of power, itself a complex determined by frequency and quality of performance. Given that I can command the performance consisting in the provision of best textual means to an end, or of items satisfying some neutral description, can I trust that the performance will be perfect, or nearly perfect, that I shall actually get the best means, or all and only those that fit the neutral description? Can I expect always to get the best performance, or always to get a less than best performance, or sometimes the best and sometimes a poor performance? The same questions might be asked of my own performances, and one who can consistently carry out or have carried out for him perfect performances is in a stronger position than one who cannot. This dimension of reliability will occupy us later at some length.[16]

An obvious dimension of power is that of *extent:* if one's control extended over the entire bibliographical universe, the extent of control would be as great as possible. The actual extent of a man's power would be specified, if this were possible, by enumerating or describing in general terms the items over which he had control, items which I shall say constitute the *field* of control. One obvious way of contrasting the situations of two people or

---

[16] In discussions of the evaluation of the performance of information retrieval or indexing systems, the quality of a response is generally graded in terms of "recall" and "precision" (the latter term having replaced, in such contexts, the term "relevance"): the "recall ratio" is the proportion of items from an "ideal" set (usually defined in terms of the notion of relevance to a request) actually produced in response to a request, the "precision ratio" being the proportion of items from the "ideal" set in the whole group of items actually produced (the relative "purity" of the response). Such quantitative notions do not suit very well the evaluation of responses to exercises of exploitative control, though they do in the case of descriptive control (though that is not, or not clearly, what is under discussion in the writings alluded to). The two factors seem of unequal and perhaps inconstant importance. If I ask for writings on Hottentots, and am given a set of which half are on Hottentots and half not, the response is clearly defective in a way, and I may or may not be dissatisfied (though I need not be dissatisfied, for some of the unrequested items may interest me). The more time and effort I

Describing and Exploiting

groups of people is by comparing the extent of their bibliographical control, the relative sizes of their fields of control, one man having more power than another simply by having power over more things. We must not hope that in practice we could make perfectly exact determinations of fields of control, but rough measures are clearly possible. The "literature" of chemistry, for instance, is vastly greater than that of symbolic logic, and control over all or most of the former is a greater power, in one dimension, than control over all or most of the latter.

A further dimension we can call *range,* though perhaps *versatility* would be more apt. The range of my power over any collection of objects corresponds to the number and variety of demands I can make on those objects. The greater the number and variety of purposes for which I can have suitable textual means provided, and the greater the number and variety of neutral descriptions in terms of which I can successfully pose requests, the greater my power over my field of control. Conversely, the more limited the repertory of requests I can make, the less my power. Ability to have identified writings specified in terms of authorship and also in terms of subject matter is a greater ability than the ability to have identified writings specified in terms of authorship alone; ability to have identified writings specified in terms of a small and "general" repertory of descriptions of subject matter is a smaller ability than it would be if the repertory were large and "specific." This dimension of power is also a complex one, to be estimated in terms both of the numbers of sorts of demand one can make, and the numbers of demands of each sort, both the varieties of discrimination possible, and the fineness of discrimination possible.

Another dimension is what we may call the dimension of *supply.* If we think of the sorts of power we might have over any collection of objects whatever, it springs to mind that the highest degree of power would be

---

must expend in sorting the requested from the unrequested items, the less satisfied I shall be. If the sorting is of a kind I can do, however, my dissatisfaction will be less than it will be if I cannot myself do the sorting. If I ask for the best textual means to some end, and am given a mixed bag of writings among which the best means is said to be included, but without being specifically identified, and if I am unable to identify it myself, then the unrequested items are more than a mere encumbrance, for they effectively conceal the requested item. Superfluous items of a sort I can recognize are a minor irritation at most; superfluous items of a sort I cannot recognize are a disaster.

The various measures for the evaluation of the performance of information retrieval systems are reviewed in John A. Swets, "Information Retrieval Systems," *Science,* 141 (19 July 1963), 245–250; attempts at evaluation are reviewed in Charles P. Bourne, "Evaluation of Indexing Systems," in *Annual Review of Information Science and Technology,* I, ed. Carlos A. Cuadra (New York, 1966), pp. 171–190.

conferred by absolute ownership. The owner of an object, if his ownership is absolute, can do what he likes with the object; he can destroy it, mutilate it, give it away, use it in any way that he likes and can. A lesser degree of power is that of having access to the object, under some conditions or none, having the right to use but not destroy, mutilate, "misuse," or dispose of the object. Restrictions on access and use are restrictions on power. The applications of this notion of power to the bibliographical situation are obvious. If I can have supplied me, or can myself get, not copies of texts but only information about the location of copies, my position is weaker than when I have access, however restricted, to copies; while if I can get or find only the description of texts, but not information about the location of copies, my position is as bad as possible in this dimension of power. I do not know that it is necessary to argue that this *is* a dimension of the powers that constitute bibliographical control. Is it not just obvious that I could not be said to have bibliographical control over a body of literature that was entirely inaccessible to me, copies of which I was never under any circumstances permitted to see? No matter how great my power over a field in other respects, if I can never directly get at those writings, my power over them is in one direction nil. We might find a flourishing publishing industry on a remote planet, whose friendly bibliographers assured us they could furnish writings answering our every desire, but if export restrictions unfortunately forbade our ever seeing any of those writings, could we be said to have effective control over their literature? At best, inability to see the writings that one could have described and evaluated in any way one liked would make one's power defective, at worst it would reduce it to zero.

Two further dimensions of power can be dismissed with brief mention. One is that of "response time": the more quickly I can do or have done what I want, the better my position. Another is that of effort: the less work is required of me in order to get what I want, the better my position, and the best position is to have to do nothing but ask. The total and accurate description of the bibliographical control available to an individual would require specification of all these things: extent and range, supply and reliability, access time and effort, and the first mentioned dimension, the "scope" or number of individuals whose textual requirements the given individual could satisfy. It would not require specification of *cost;* we neither increase nor decrease a power by making it expensive, or by making it free. Exactly the same power might be had by a pauper who paid nothing and a billionaire who paid billions. Having described a man's power, we may go on to

Describing and Exploiting 39

ask who bears the costs of his exercising that power, but we could completely describe the power without ever raising that question. Of course one's wealth usually determines the amount of power one can attain: the poor man lacks the power to attain certain powers, if the essential means to the acquisition of power is money, as it usually is. But if bibliographical control cannot be attained without money, and might be lost without continuous expenditure of money, still the extent of power can be estimated quite apart from questions of cost.

As estimates of amounts of power are independent of considerations of the cost of acquiring and maintaining power (and of considerations of who pays), so they are independent of considerations of the means through which power is exercised, or the ways in which one comes to have power. One who has power over a set of objects may exercise that power directly or indirectly, and if indirectly then through a system of arrangements involving only people, or only instruments, or both people and instruments. The description of a power is the description of what one can do or have done, of the results of exercise of the power rather than of the form of the exercise. Two people might in principle have the same sort and degree of power over identical fields, but exercise that power by means of the most dissimilar arrangements. Nothing in the notion of power or control implies that he who has control has himself any particular knowledge or skills. What you can do simply in virtue of your own knowledge and skill, I may be able to do in virtue of what I can ask others to do for me. In the bibliographical world, as in others, one may be a witless king, powerful because of the knowledge and skills of one's subjects. The witless king may, of course, fail to appreciate the extent of his power, lack the capacity to utilize his power, or lack interest in doing so. This is true as well in the bibliographical world. Of the things I could do or have done if I wanted, only a fraction are things I am aware I could do, and only a fraction are things I shall ever want to do. And there are requests I could have met, that *would* be met were I to make them, that nevertheless I never *could* make, my own ignorance (and other characteristics) effectively preventing me from ever entertaining or formulating them. The power available to a man, the power that in one sense he *has,* must then be sharply distinguished from the power he will ever care to use.

If I had the greatest conceivable degree of exploitative control, I would be able to have the best means to my and everyone else's ends supplied instantaneously, effortlessly, with absolute reliability, the supply consisting of the most suitable copy or performance in the bibliographical universe. If I had the greatest conceivable degree of descriptive control, I could have supplied, under analogous conditions, items satisfying or fitting any neutral or non-evaluative description whatever. If I had such powers, it would mean that everything that could possibly be known about the characteristics and interrelations of texts, the textual and intellectual history of each work, was known and could be made known to me. More than this: everything would be known about all individuals, or everything that need be known in order to identify the best textual means to every end they might conceivably set themselves. This would, in effect, be to have not only the entire bibliographical universe, but an omniscient bibliographer and psychologist at one's disposal. Bibliographical control implies access to knowledge about texts, and their exemplars, and in its highest degree implies that knowledge about texts that is represented in the notion of complete *mastery* of a body of texts. But this mastery is not only knowledge of the contents of texts and the historical and other relations among texts; it is knowledge of all the uses to which texts can be put, by all possible users in all possible circumstances. We shall never, in this world, have such control; but the ideal is an intelligible one.[17]

---

[17] It is true a fortiori, and hardly in need of mention, that no single device, however complex, could be constructed that would give anyone who had access to it complete bibliographical control. No "universal bibliographical machine" is possible, even in principle. No matter how large a store of "information" a machine contained, the machine could not be such as to give, for any arbitrary demand, made by any person whomever, the best textual means to the solution of the problem or question posed, or the writings satisfying some description presented. The finite store of information about any set of writings could not answer every possible question about those writings, for there are not a finite number of possible questions, and the possible questions cannot all be reduced, by any conceivable procedure, to a finite list of "basic" questions. Of course an omniscient bibliographer and engineer could provide us with a machine that would answer all the questions we in fact ever *will* want to put.

On the impossibility of an "ideal" bibliographical machine, see further Y. Bar-Hillel, "The Mechanisation of Literature Searching," in *Mechanisation of Thought Processes*, National Physical Laboratory Symposium no. 10 (London, 1959), II, pp. 789–807.

CHAPTER III

RELEVANCE

IT HAS BEEN CLAIMED that "the key concept of any proper theory of information storage and retrieval is that of relevance";[1] and it may be claimed that that concept is also the key concept in any proper account ("theory" is too lofty a word for the analysis here attempted) of bibliographical control. There are so many obvious similarities between the study of information retrieval and the study of bibliographical control that it would be surprising if what was the central concept of one study were not also at least one of the central concepts of the other study. Perhaps, instead of chat about best means to ends, and about calling out items satisfying arbitrary neutral descriptions, we should have stated our ideal at once in terms of relevance, and have devoted our energies to an attempt at arriving at a "procedure for actually establishing a quantitative measure for relevance,"[2] a way of giving numerical values to writings instead of talking so imprecisely about the value or utility of writings as means to ends.

But is it indeed clear that the notion of relevance is suitable to serve as the basic notion in an analysis of bibliographical control? I do not mean the *word* "relevance," for a word can be defined as one pleases. Perhaps there are notions, with which we might be made acquainted by means of a novel definition of the word "relevance," which would turn out to be more suitable than those we have used. But if so, then the question is not one of the suitability or centrality of the concept of relevance, but of some other concept to which, for some reason, the word "relevance" is attached. If one claims that the concept of relevance is central to a study, then we are entitled to assume that what is being claimed to be central is a concept with which we are already familiar, namely the concept conventionally associated with the word "relevance," and not some other concept.

Now it is the frequent complaint of writers on information storage and retrieval that the notion of relevance, which they take to be central

---

[1] M. E. Maron, "A Logician's View of Language-Data Processing," in Paul Garvin, ed., *Natural Language and the Computer* (New York, 1963), pp. 146–147. See also M. E. Maron and J. L. Kuhns, "On Relevance, Probabilistic Indexing and Information Retrieval," *Journal of the Association for Computing Machinery*, 7 (1960), pp. 220–221 et passim. Similar claims are found very frequently in the literature of information retrieval.

[2] Maron, op. cit., p. 147.

to their study, is a fuzzy and obscure one, one which requires clearing up, making precise, *explication*, if it is to play its centrol role well.[3] What this requires may be seen by reference to one of the classic accounts of the process of explication, that of Carnap in *Logical Foundations of Probability*.[4]

The task of *explication* consists in transforming a given more or less inexact concept into an exact one or, rather, in replacing the first by the second. We call the given concept (or the term used for it) the *explicandum*, and the exact concept proposed to take the place of the first (or the term proposed for it) the *explicatum*.

The aim, in the process of explication, is to formulate a concept that is in the first place *similar* to the explicandum, in that "in most cases in which the explicandum has so far been used, the explicatum can be used," that is in the second place *exact*, that is in the third place *fruitful*, "that is, useful for the formulation of many universal statements" (empirical laws or logical theorems), and that is, finally, as simple as possible, which means as simple as the first three requirements permit. I do not know that students of information storage and retrieval expect to use an explicated concept of relevance in the formulation of many empirical laws or logical theorems; the intended use of the concept is humbler than that. But it seems obvious that a satisfactory explicatum of "relevance" would have to be *applicable* and *useful* in practice; we may, I think, take these terms as giving the appropriate sense of *fruitful* in this context.

Prior to the attempt to discover a suitable explicatum for a concept, there is necessary a preliminary clarification; we cannot do better than quote Carnap further:[5]

There is a temptation to think that, since the explicandum cannot be given in exact terms anyway, it does not matter much how we formulate the problem.

---

[3] Maron, op. cit., and Maron and Kuhns, op. cit., speak specifically of the need for explication; others only complain of the obscurity or "subjectivity" or general fuzziness of the term. See Arthur D. Little, Inc., *Centralization and Documentation* (Cambridge, Mass., 1963), p. 20; Cyril W. Cleverdon, *Report on the Testing and Analysis of an Investigation into the Comparative Efficiency of Indexing Systems* (Cranfield, 1962), p. 51 ("relevance is, in the present state of the art [sic], a purely subjective assessment"); *Summary of Study Conference on Evaluation of Document Searching Systems and Procedures*, ... 1964 (Washington, D.C.: National Science Foundation [1964?]), especially leaves 7-10.

[4] Rudolf Carnap, *Logical Foundations of Probability* (Chicago, 1950), p. 3. All of Chapter I on explication should be read. Chapter VI attempts a formalization of the concepts of relevance and irrelevance.

[5] Carnap, op. cit., p. 4.

But this would be quite wrong. On the contrary, since even in the best case we cannot reach full exactness, we must, in order to prevent the discussion of the problem from becoming entirely futile, do all we can to make at least practically clear what is meant as the explicandum.... Even though the terms in question are unsystematic, inexact terms, there are means for reaching a relatively good mutual understanding as to their intended meaning. An indication of the meaning with the help of some examples for its intended use and other examples for uses not now intended can help the understanding.... All explanations of this kind serve only to make clear what is meant as the explicandum; they do not yet supply an explication, say a definition of the explicatum; they belong still to the formulation of the problem, not yet to the construction of an answer.

Now I do not think it would be claimed that any precise, exact, and *fruitful,* that is, applicable and useful, explications of the concept of relevance have been produced as yet, that could demand to be the central concepts in a theory either of information storage and retrieval or of bibliographical control. But further, I do not think that even the necessary preliminary clarification has been sufficiently attempted. It is not, that is, even clear *what* familiar notion it is for which explications are proposed. Let us, therefore, put ourselves in the position of one who has at his disposal only the ordinary, everyday, imprecise notion of relevance, and who is asked to say whether that notion looks like something which, when suitably explicated, would serve as a central or key concept for the understanding of bibliographical control. Let us try to "make at least practically clear what is meant as the explicandum," so that we can try to decide whether that notion is one we should work to explicate, and substitute for those already employed in explaining types of bibliographical control.

The dictionary tells us only that what is relevant is what has "bearing on," what is "connected with, pertinent to, the matter in hand"; but we can, I think, be rather more precise about the sort of bearing, connection, pertinence. The heart of the notion of relevance can be reached simply by reflection on the sorts of things customarily and correctly said to be relevant: objections, arguments, considerations, as well as "facts" and "information." Anything that tends to sustain or overthrow a conclusion or an hypothesis, anything that can properly be cited as evidence for or against a claim, has relevance to the conclusion, hypothesis, or claim, and is the more relevant, the more heavily it weighs for or against. Irrelevant objections or considerations are those that count neither for nor against, that are in that sense "neither here nor there." Relevant objections and considerations are those that are either here or there, either for or against. Relevance is thus a matter of evidential or argumentative status; that which adds to the weight of the evidence for or against an hypothesis is more or less relevant, as it adds more or less weight; that which adds no weight on either side is irrelevant. The relevance or irrelevance of an item (here always a statement or set of statements) is a matter of logic, not of sentiment or "mere subjective opinion" as is sometimes claimed,[6] a matter to be determined a priori rather than by observation or experiment. Appraisal of statements as relevant or irrelevant to an hypothesis or claim is an exercise of judgment, and inability to appraise relevance is a mark of silliness or irrationality, though inability to estimate exactly how relevant a statement or set of statements is to an hypothesis is not necessarily so, since the notion does not come equipped with the means for making such estimates. But the theory of relevance has been studied by logicians as a chapter in the general theory of inductive logic, the logic of the confirmation of hypotheses, and in some of those studies an attempt is made to provide means of quantitative estimation of degrees of relevance.[7] If one wants an explication of the ordinary concept of relevance, the writings of inductive logic are the place to look for it.

This notion of relevance, the notion of the evidential status of statements in relation to particular hypotheses or claims or conclusions, is clearly insufficient for describing the powers we wish to include in the notion of bibliographical control. If, in the exercise of my power, I ask for all the published writings of Rudolf Carnap, and am given copies of each of them, I am not given something relevant to my hypothesis or claim, for I presented none. If I ask for something that will best help me understand the notion of "ego-strength," and am given a writing which does in fact help me understand that notion, I am not given something relevant to my hypothesis, for I presented no hypothesis. Of course I might *have* an hypothesis, to which some of the statements in the writing were relevant, but the relation between that hypothesis and those statements is not like the relation of my request to what fulfills it.

Perhaps the notion of relevance, as known to us before explication, has application to statements which constitute answers to questions, and to things produced in response to a request. Clearly, some statements are

---

[6] See note 3 above. Compare *Webster's Dictionary of Synonyms* (Springfield, Mass., 1951), s.v. *relevance*: "That is *relevant* which has any traceable connection, especially logical connection, with the thing under consideration ..." But I am not supposing lexicographers to be infallible.

[7] See note 4 above.

related to a question in ways others are not, in that they are statements which favor one or another possible answer to the question; they are such that, if true, they support or confirm one or another possible answer to the question, or disconfirm others. It is a recognized rhetorical device to answer a question "by implication" rather than directly, by saying (and suggesting that there is nothing else significant to say) something from which follows, obviously and naturally, the answer one wishes to convey. Instead of saying, when requested to do so, what I think of a person's honesty, I might reply: "He has served three terms for embezzlement and two for forgery," from which my opinion, failing any other remarks on my part, can sufficiently be gathered.

This question-relevance, as we might call it, parallels the other relevance, in that it is a matter of evidential bearing to a particular hypothesis or claim, assertion of which would constitute answering the question directly, whether correctly or incorrectly. In order for a statement to be relevant to a question, it must be relevant in the first sense to some other statement which would count as a possible direct answer to the question. Recognizing the question-relevance of a statement involves two moments or factors: recognizing the relevance of the statement to some other statement (in the first sense of "relevance"), and recognizing the latter as a possible direct answer to the question.[8] So relevance is a complicated relationship in this second sense, a "relative product" of two other relationships: a statement X is relevant to a question Y just in case there is some other statement Z which is itself a direct answer to Y (whether correct or incorrect is not important), and to which X is relevant in the first sense. If we are given, in answer to a question, a statement which we

---

[8] Whether a direct answer to a question could, in a degenerate or trivial sense, be called relevant to the question would depend on whether a statement could be called relevant to itself. Since every statement follows logically from itself, one might argue that every direct answer is question-relevant, since from the direct answer follows something, namely the answer itself, which is also a direct answer. But no statement *is* evidence for itself; I cannot, for instance, show that my opinion that it will rain tomorrow is a likely one, simply by reasserting my opinion. And so we can argue that no direct answer to a question is itself question-relevant to that very question (though it might be question-relevant to some other question). I am assuming that it is possible in principle to give a syntactic or purely formal characterization of the notion of direct answer, an assumption consistent, so far as I know, with contemporary linguistic theory. For a formal treatment of the logic of question and answer, see David Harrah, *Communication: A Logical Model* (Cambridge, Mass., 1963), and works referred to therein. My "question-relevance" is wider in scope than his "partial answer" (pp. 39 ff.).

recognize as not a direct answer, we may still judge the relevance of the statement; but if we are given what we recognize as a direct answer, whether correct or incorrect, then the question of relevance does not arise. If you ask me my age and I say that it is eighty-five, a palpable falsehood, you would have no occasion to wonder about the relevance of my answer to your request, though you would wonder why I bother to lie. The answer is recognizable as an answer, though incorrect, and a question of relevance is neither appropriate nor intelligible. If I had said, however, "I remember the Panay," you might perhaps want to say that this, though not a direct answer, was yet relevant in that it gave you a way of arriving at a minimum age. And if we are given a direct answer to a question, we may of course go on to ask what reasons there are for thinking the answer correct, to which question the answer must take the form of statements which are relevant to the first answer, and will not be recognized *as* answers unless recognized *as* relevant to the first answer. But that complex relationship does not show that relevance is the same as the relation of question to answer, only that in order to recognize some statements as answers, we must recognize them as relevant to some previous answers.

We may take it, I think, that neither relevance or question-relevance, as we understand those notions before explication, is suitable as a single central concept in an analysis of bibliographical control. But what of the relation of a request to things provided in response to the request? Certainly that relationship is not known under the name of "relevance." If I ask a butcher for a leg of lamb, and he gives me one, I do not congratulate him on his excellent estimates of degrees of relevance, and indeed I cannot even understand what it would be like to do so. For he has not given me what is relevant to my request, he has simply given me what I asked for. If instead he gives me a shoulder of mutton, I do not complain, and indeed I would be baffled by the suggestion that I should complain, that he had given me something irrelevant to my request; for he would simply have given me something other than what I requested, something that did not fit the description I presented in my request. "Fitting a description" and "relevant" are not synonymous or even coextensive in application. They are similar in that both allow of degrees: statements are more or less relevant to an hypothesis, things come more or less close to fitting a description. But this similarity is insufficient to make the two notions interchangeable; providing a more accurate description of a thing is not the same as providing a more relevant statement about the thing, or a more relevant description of the thing, though by providing a more accurate description of a thing we might provide ourselves with statements more relevant to some hypothesis.

The reason for resisting the use of the notion of relevance in speaking of the relation of request to things provided in response to the request is not, of course, that "relevant" simply cannot be applied to things other than statements or by extension to what contains statements. For people will say things like "Certain biological capacities and traits...often become particularly relevant to the demands set up by new roles....." But when a trait, capacity, thing is said to be relevant, it is relevance in the sense of causal connection or statistical correlation, so that knowing about the thing that is relevant gives us reason for some particular beliefs about that to which it is relevant, thus reflecting the original sense of "relevance," that of evidential status.

There are other contexts in which relevance is talked of: for instance, decisions and the considerations which should enter into the making of particular decisions (where relevance is a matter of support for one decision over another) and evaluations and the considerations which should influence or determine particular evaluations (where relevance is a matter of support for one verdict over another). But reflection on such contexts will not, I think, support a claim for the centrality of the familiar, unexplicated concept of relevance in an account of bibliographical control. To say of something that it fits a certain description is not to employ the concept of relevance, and unless one wants to deny that the ability to identify items that fit some description is the sort of thing that could be an exercise of bibliographical control, he will have to admit that, as it is now, the notion of relevance is not a sufficiently general one to serve as a substitute for the two different notions that define our two different sorts of control.

The sense, or senses, or "relevance" indicated above might be said to belong to the *logical* concept of relevance. Perhaps there is another concept associated with the word "relevance" that would serve as a single central concept in an account of bibliographical control. I think we can easily discover another, quite different, way in which the word "relevance" is at least sometimes used. There is a fairly clear distinction between looking for evidence that will favor or disfavor an hypothesis, and looking on the other hand for anything that will *suggest* hypotheses without necessarily providing evidence for or against them; and what suggests an hypothesis might be said to be relevant. There is a fairly clear distinction between looking for what will answer a question, and (perhaps knowing that nothing will do so) looking for what may suggest a way of answering the question, what will help one formulate what may turn out to be the answer one seeks: and what is thus helpful might be termed relevant. Relevance in these cases amounts to being "auailefull," as an old writer has it.[9] But it is relevance, not to an hypothesis or claim or theory, but to a problem or inquiry, and what is relevant is what helps solve the problem or further the inquiry. We must not lean too heavily on the terms "problem" and "inquiry." A person who has a doubt is puzzled, is confused, does not understand some matter, may count as relevant whatever helps resolve his doubt, solve his puzzlement, clarify his confusion, provide understanding.

If relevance in the earlier, logical, sense was basically a relationship between an hypothesis or claim and what tells for or against it, in the present sense it is a relationship between, for instance, a doubt and what helps set it at rest, a perplexity and what resolves it, an unclarity and what reduces it, and (not least) a problem and what helps solve it. In this second sense, relevance does not appear to differ from utility as means to an end, and the most relevant textual matter could scarcely be other than the best textual means to an end. If a text is relevant, in this sense, to a problem, it is because it helps solve that problem; but what is this other than being a textual means to the end of solving that problem? Evidently the best textual means for my purpose may not be the best

---

[9] *Oxford English Dictionary*, s.v. *relevance*. Arthur Andersen & Co., New York, *Final Report: Research Study of Criteria and Procedures for Evaluating Scientific Information Retrieval Systems*, Prepared for Office of Science Information Service, National Science Foundation ... (Contract NSF–C218) (March, 1962), leaf 98: "An object is relevant to a user's need if it supplies him with information that helps him fulfill that need." Gerard Salton, letter to editor, *American Documentation*, 16 (1965), 341: there are really two distinct uses of "relevance," of which the first "involves a judgment made by a user of an information system when he decides that a given document retrieved in answer to a search request is either useful to him (relevant) or not useful (irrelevant)." The second use is not defined, but perhaps was meant to be explained as "actually useful" as opposed to "thought to be useful." In experiments carried out at Western Reserve University, subjects were asked to judge both the relevance ("the degree to which the document bears on or has application to the research you have heard described") and the usefulness ("by usefulness we mean the degree to which the document would be useful to you as an individual") of documents. The distinction is not usually drawn so sharply in such tests. See *A Field Experimental Approach to the Study of Relevance Assessments in Relation to Document Searching, Formal Progress Report No. 2*, NSF Contract No. C–423, Center for Documentation and Communication Research, School of Library Science, Western Reserve University (Cleveland, 1966), leaf 16.

textual means for your purpose, even if our purposes are the same; but equally, what is relevant in this sense to my problem, what helps me solve my problem, may not be relevant to your problem, even if we have the same problem. It is hard to see a significant difference between the two notions.

But if the second sense of "relevance" is not significantly different from our notion of textual means to an end, it is significantly different from the first, logical, sense of relevance. There need be no relationship known to logic between a text and a problem it helps someone solve. One may seek to understand a phenomenon, not in the way of looking for an explanatory theory, but for something that will help one to what is vaguely called "insight"; and there is no telling what may occasion a flash of insight. Human society might suddenly seem "understandable" on the basis of something one read about machines or animal ecology or theology, and what one read might then be said to have been relevant, i.e., helpful, for producing that understanding. What is helpful is what does in fact help, whether or not it ought to, whether or not we could ever have reasonably expected it to, and however it does help. Further, relevance in this sense is at least a three-term relationship, between text, problem (or doubt, inquiry, etc.) and person (and we should almost certainly have to include a fourth term, time); we could not speak of a text being relevant to a problem *simpliciter* unless we tacitly assumed it would help anyone, at any time, who had that problem. The first, logical, sense of "relevance" is, on the other hand, an ineradicably normative or deontic one, and one that is not relative to persons and times. What is relevant to a thesis or question or decision or evaluation, in the first sense, is not just that which someone thinks worth mention, but that which *ought* to be taken into account. A person's beliefs and decisions and evaluations may in fact be influenced by a host of factors that we say are irrelevant because they ought not be influences. We do not first determine the relevance of a statement or consideration and then say that it ought to be taken into account, as if it were a conclusion we had reached on the basis of experience or observation that in general it was a good thing to take relevant considerations into account. Rather, saying something is relevant is already, in a way, saying it ought to be considered. Talk of relevance, in the first sense, is talk that is deeply impregnated with oughts and musts, with appraisals and demands. And these appraisals and demands are quite impersonal; if a fact or consideration is relevant to an hypothesis or evaluation, it is relevant all the time, for everybody. "Relevant for me" is, in this sense of "relevance," as senseless as "true for me."

The difference between the two concepts of relevance is so great that it is apparent that no single explicatum could replace our present vague talk of relevance, for we are talking of at least two quite different things.[10] An explicatum that preserved the normative character and impersonality of the first concept would not do as a replacement for the second concept. But the first concept is, as noted earlier, properly the province of the inductive logician; and I think we may take it that the second concept is the one that is to be explicated for use in the theory of information storage and retrieval. Now this second concept, being practically equivalent to our concept of textual means to an end, must therefore be as central as the latter to the study of bibliographical control. We may say that the notion of exploitative control utilizes that notion, under a different name, and as I am claiming in this work that exploitative control is one of the two basic sorts of bibliographical control, I must also claim that relevance, in the second sense, is one of the basic notions of the study of bibliographical control. Of course relevance in the first sense is a key notion as well; for one of the primary features of a writing on which its utility depends is its containing material relevant in the first sense to hypotheses, decisions, evaluations of one sort or another. But if both concepts of relevance enter into an account of bibliographical control, neither one alone, nor both together, can be sufficient for a proper account of bibliographical control. In particular, descriptive control cannot be elucidated in terms of textual utilities or means to ends, or in terms of the logical concept of relevance. To mention only one sort of case, there is a difference between a writing's being *on* a given topic and a writing's being *relevant to* the study or investigation of that topic, in either sense of "relevance." If I ask for all the writings there are on Carnap's notions of inductive logic, and get them, I shall not yet have got all the writings containing material relevant (in the first sense) to the study of those notions, and may have got many that are not relevant (in the second sense) to *my* study, since they may tell me only what I already know, or what I see to be mistaken or absurd, and so on.

If the second concept of relevance is the one that is more important for

---

[10] I am not claiming that it is always easy to tell which, if either, of the two senses of "relevance" is being employed on any given occasion. Frequently both make equally good sense in a context, since the relevant (in the first sense) is likely to be useful (i.e., relevant in the second sense).

our study, and for the study of information storage and retrieval, what of the claim that it is fuzzy and obscure, requiring explication before it will play its part well? The claim seems hardly convincing; for surely we know quite well what it is for a text to be useful as a means to various ends, and we know quite well that there are endless different ways in which texts can be useful, and we know that the possible utilities of a writing cannot all be recognized at a given time.[11] We do not stand in grievous need of a more refined *notion* of relevance in the sense of textual utility as means to end, though we would certainly like to be shown how to detect utilities. If an explicator of "relevance" proposes to give us new means for recognizing the potential utilities of writings, he is much to be encouraged. If he proposes to establish a procedure for measuring the utilities of texts, we may legitimately be skeptical. The gift of a procedure for assigning numbers to writings, unless it represents an actual increase in our knowledge of the utilities of texts, is likely to be a trivial, if perhaps amusing, gift. We are frequently able to say that one item is likely to be better than another as means to some end; but a general procedure by which we could determine that one writing was, say, exactly three times as useful as another (for particular purposes, persons, times, presumably) would constitute such an astonishing advance in our knowledge of people and texts and indeed everything else in the universe that we may doubt that a mere mortal could ever discover one.

After all this is said, it is still open to the friend of relevance to say that there is no harm in taking the unexplicated, inexact term "relevance" as the basic one in studies of information retrieval and bibliographical control. One wants, he may say, to have a *single* term to use for the relation between a text and a request whenever the text satisfies the request to some degree, or would satisfy the request were it produced. Whether the word "relevance" is a perfectly suitable one or not, no harm could be done if it were made quite clear that "relevance" was being used for *any* of the relations between text and request that make a text satisfactory in relation to a request. And one might then propose to explicate the notion of relevance in this new, extended sense of the word.[12]

---

[11] See above, Chapter II, pp. 33–34.
[12] See Cyril Cleverdon et al., *Factors Determining the Performance of Indexing Systems, Vol. I: Design, Part 1: Text* (Cranfield, 1966), pp. 21 ff., 123 ff. Participants in one of the Aslib Cranfield Research Project's experiments were asked to "assess the relevance" of papers to questions posed by the participants, in the following way:
Mark as (1) references which are a complete answer to the question....
Mark as (2) references of a high degree of relevance, the lack of which would have

If one did so extend the term, it must be clear that now the word "relevance" would have come to be equivalent to the word "satisfactory"; the most satisfactory texts, in relation to a request, would be the most relevant, and vice versa. Using the term "relevance" in this way, one could of course claim that it was central to one's study. But the claim would be a trivial one. For one could now say that the aim of information storage and retrieval systems was always and simply the provision of relevant writings, and only relevant writings, in response to requests; and analogously for bibliographical control, which would be the ability to have such writings produced. But this, while true, is as little informative as can be imagined; it means simply that the aim of such systems is to satisfy requests made on them, and that bibliographical control is the ability to get what one asks for. Only use of the word "relevance" masks the

> made the research impracticable or would have resulted in a considerable amount of extra work.
> Mark as (3) references which were useful, either as general background to the work or as suggesting methods of tackling certain aspects of the work.
> Mark as (4) references of minimum interest, for example, those that have been included from a historical viewpoint.
> Mark as (5) references of no interest.

The note was appended to the instructions: "It is appreciated that it is not easy to do this objectively, for personal considerations tend to influence judgment." The experimenters say (p. 16) that "no-one is more aware [than they] that relevance is a shifting notion, certainly between individuals and often for the same individuals at different times." If it is a "shifting" notion, it may be because they have made it so. If writings may be relevant in some degree because containing an answer to a set question, or containing perhaps necessary ancillary or operational information, or containing *useful* information generally or *suggesting* methods of solving problems, then it is hardly to be wondered at that different people should make different "assessments of relevance."

That "personal considerations tend to influence judgment" is an odd remark in the context of instructions to estimate interest and usefulness; for what could these be expected to mean except interest and utility to the experimental subject, or else his guesses about interest and utility to his colleagues? But none of the five possible marks seems to fit the case in which a man is glad to get a paper because it is *on* topic X and he has asked for papers on topic X. I suspect it is only by inadvertence that such a case was not provided for; for it is quite clear that "relevance" is here being used simply as a substitute for "satisfactoriness," that "highly relevant" means nothing beyond "eminently satisfactory." On the basis of the following passage, I take it that Professor Rees would agree with me:

> Since we cannot assess the covert satisfaction or impact of retrieval systems on the part of users it is necessary to consider phenomena which are overt [sic] and reasonably explicit. For this reason, relevance is used as the criterion measure to quantify the phenomenon involved when individuals (users) judge the relationship, utility, importance, degree of match, fit, proximity, appropriateness, closeness, pertinence, value or bearing of documents or document representations to an information requirement, need, question, statement, description of research, treatment, etc.—Alan M. Rees, *The Relevance of Relevance to the Testing and Evaluation of Document Retrieval Systems* (Cleveland: Center for Documentation and Communication Research, School of Library Science, Western Reserve University, 1966?), leaf 3.

triviality of the claim, and misleadingly suggests that a much more interesting (but also false) claim is being made. But it is also clear that it is not now the *concept* of relevance that is central to one's study, but the concept of satisfying a request. There seems little point in trying to *explicate* the notion of satisfying a request; that notion does not need to be replaced by a similar but more exact one. What is needed is rather an analysis of the different *sorts* of ways in which writings can satisfy requests, and the devising of better means of recognizing and recording the various utilities of writings. Writings may satisfy a request because relevant, in either of the senses distinguished above; but there are other ways of being satisfactory, and uncounted numbers of ways of being relevant, in either sense. Use of the term "relevant" in place of the term "satisfactory" can only confuse, not clarify, the study of bibliographical control, however it may be in the study of information storage and retrieval.

Let us now summarize this lengthy discussion. It is claimed that the notion of relevance is the key or central concept in any proper theory of information storage and retrieval, and that, if true, makes it likely that the same notion would be central in a proper account of bibliographical control. It is also claimed that the notion is, as used in ordinary speech, vague and inexact and in need of explication, that is, replacement by an exact concept. Now one way of proving the centrality of the concept of relevance would be by presenting a description of an exactly formulated concept which was seen to be a fruitful (applicable and useful) one, one which by its merits pushed all other contenders from the field. This has not, to my knowledge, been done.

Another way of proving the centrality of that concept would be by a preliminary examination of the familiar vague concept, showing that it was already the chief contender, that it was clear, by reflection on its customary use, that a precise explication of that concept would be more likely to be fruitful than any other. But this is what I think the preceding discussion has shown to be false. There is not a single ordinary concept of relevance, but at least two of them; and while both enter into a satisfactory account of bibliographical control, neither can claim to be *the* central concept. It is not true that all the varieties of bibliographical control can be described in terms of either notion of relevance. By using the word "relevance" with the meaning of being satisfactory in relation to a request, one can assert, quite trivially, that the word, but not the concept, of relevance, is central to the study of bibliographical control. Both the senses of relevance are indeed important for our study, and one of them is in effect equivalent to our notion of textual means to an end. In that sense, what is required is not an explication of the concept, which is clear enough, but better means of recognizing and recording the utilities of writings. In order to avoid possible confusions, it would be much preferable to use three terms for three notions, to speak of relevance in the first sense, or logical relevance, and of textual means to ends, and of satisfactoriness, instead of using "relevance" for all these three notions.

Chapter IV

BIBLIOGRAPHICAL INSTRUMENTS AND THEIR SPECIFICATIONS

I CANNOT TELL how much bibliographical control I have or could have simply by introspection, by memory of past successes and failures, or by flexing my muscles. To discover what I can or might do if I would, I must discover what arrangements there are of which I can take advantage, what bibliographical instruments, personal skills and knowledge, and institutions are at my disposal. Let us see what can be said, abstractly and generally, about the features of available apparatus and personnel on which would depend the strength or weakness of my bibliographical situation, as a necessary preliminary to considering how one would decide on the satisfactoriness or unsatisfactoriness of a situation. Let us for the present ignore people and institutions, and think only of instruments. We will suppose ourselves setting out to make an inventory of the available bibliographical apparatus, and to see what strength that inventory gives him to whom it is available.

What is to count as an item in that inventory or repertory of instruments is not, however, an obvious thing. Which objects are bibliographical instruments? All the things which can be used in the location of textual means to the attainment of some end, or in the identification of writings answering some description or other? To call anything that might be used, more or less successfully, for a bibliographical purpose a bibliographical instrument would be rather like calling everything a hammer that could be used, more or less successfully, to do one of the things that hammers are for, and so counting into the world inventory of hammers various rocks and pieces of scrap metal. Not quite like that, however; for a given item might serve a single bibliographical purpose that was served by no other instrument, and so have a unique value, which might also be its only value. Any text that refers in any way to any other text or copy of some text might be considered a potential bibliographical instrument; the set of texts referring in some way to other texts and copies might be identified with the entire potential bibliographical apparatus, which would then be a very sizable portion of the whole bibliographical universe. This is not itself an absurd idea, for reference librarians talk of their libraries' entire collections as constituting their reference collections, and what serves as a reference collection might be expected to serve as a bibliographical one as well.

Within the potential bibliographical apparatus are works of specialized function, designed to serve primarily as bibliographical instruments and only incidentally as anything else: their primary aim is to list and describe other writings. The simplest of these to recognize are those that are simply lists of writings (works, texts, or copies), limited to items in the possession of some institution or person (and so called catalogs), or not so limited (and so called, generally, bibliographies).[1] To describe something as a mere list suggests that barely enough information is given about each item listed to distinguish it from the others listed; lists in which more than that minimum of information is given are sometimes called "descriptive lists." We shall have no need of a detailed classification of bibliographical instruments, and so shall not decide at what point a work primarily devoted to the description and perhaps evaluation of writings ceases to be a mere list and becomes something else, a true "descriptive bibliography" or perhaps a sort of literary history. The more information given about each item, the less likely we are to call the work a list, and the further a work departs from the

---

[1] It would be pointless to dispute with those who wish to reserve the title of "bibliography" to works in which texts or copies are described according to some very high and exacting standard of descriptive fullness. For denunciation of the practice, here followed, of using "bibliography" for simple lists of writings, see Fredson Bowers, *Principles of Bibliographical Description* (Princeton, 1949), chap. I. It would be equally pointless to quarrel with one who wants to be particularly modest about bibliography, for instance, Roy Stokes, for whom "... a bibliography, in the correct sense of the term, is an uncritical listing of all the books and materials within the coverage of the bibliography."—*Bibliographical Control and Service* (London, 1965), p. 30. One sees the point of the modesty: "... whereas the bibliographer in his own right is capable of producing a bibliography *because* it is uncritical, a subject specialist is essential if the listing is to be critical, based on an analysis or understanding of the subject matter" (loc. cit.). I see no reason to think that one who does not understand a subject matter can even produce an adequate uncritical list (see below). If he could, who would be interested in his product? Meyriat suggests an answer: "The compiler of a scientific bibliography can be asked to list only such works as make some genuine and original contribution to scientific knowledge. But in order to single out such works the author must obviously be as well qualified as the best specialists in the field of study concerned. In other words, a good specialized bibliographer of this kind must be a specialist who is willing to give up much of his time to analysing the thoughts of others instead of thinking for himself."—Jean Meyriat, *Report on the General Principles Governing International Bibliographical Work*, UNESCO/CUA/82 (Paris, 1957), p. 13. The uncritical bibliographer may compile long lists of trivia, and fail to recognize the truly significant writings because he knows too little. Courses in bibliographical method might make a person a bibliographer, in Stokes' sense of the term; they could not do so, in Meyriat's sense of the term. But courses in bibliographical method cannot be guaranteed to make anyone a *good* Stokesean bibliographer, for there is little to teach, if much to learn.

Bibliographical Instruments 57

typographical and literary conventions exhibited in "mere lists," and the closer it approximates to the typographical and literary conventions of plain expository prose, the less likely we are to think of it as a bibliographical instrument at all. But the essential characteristic of a bibliographical instrument is that it consists entirely or primarily of descriptions of works, texts, and copies, and if a work which is plainly no list consists entirely or primarily of such descriptions, then it is identical in substance, if not in style or typographical layout, with what are plainly bibliographies or catalogs, and so counts as a bibliographical instrument, in the sense of one with a narrowly specialized function.

Many works that do not consist entirely or primarily of descriptions of writings are more valuable as bibliographical instruments than any specialized instrument, but because they lack the predominant bibliographical purpose, do not fall into the class of what we can call the formal bibliographical apparatus. That formal apparatus consists of bibliographies, lists of abstracts, catalogs (published and unpublished) of collections of writings, inventories and calendars of manuscripts, book review journals, guides to literatures and to repositories of copies, indexes to periodicals, review articles, and (now or in the future) bibliographical machines or the physical apparatus (such as reels of tape) that make machines into bibliography-producing machines.

To this vaguely defined class of instruments let us add those detachable but undetached bibliographical sections of, or appendices to, works of primarily non-bibliographical purpose, lists which are neither "separately published" nor "bibliographically independent." By "detachable" I mean, lists that would be intelligible if detached from the body of the text they supplement, a condition not fulfilled by many "lists of references" and "bibliographies" attached to non-bibliographical works. A simple list of "works cited in the text" or "works referred to" or "works consulted" is frequently unintelligible apart from the writing it supplements, in that one would not understand what was listed or why; but it would be mad to exclude from the most formal part of the apparatus those frequently immense and scholarly bibliographies that accompany treatises of one sort or another, that happen never to be printed or distributed apart from the text they accompany, but which outweigh in importance a thousand other lists. There are many other detachable pieces of text that, taken separately, can be considered part of the formal apparatus, for instance, tables of contents and indexes which, though they refer only to parts of particular texts or volumes, are still intelligible apart from the texts or volumes of which they are a part and the contents of which they describe.

As the informal bibliographical apparatus, that is, all the potential apparatus except the formal part, will receive little attention in what follows, it should be emphasized here, even at the danger of stridency, that that apparatus may frequently be far more valuable than any part of the formal apparatus, detached and detachable. Insofar as the parts of the informal apparatus refer to other works and specifically evaluate or reply to or build on other writings, they add links in the complicated network of bibliographical connections, a network the tracing of which in the informal apparatus may be more valuable, if more time-consuming, than any use of the formal apparatus. Nor do the bibliographical functions of the informal apparatus merely duplicate those of the formal apparatus. The weight and trustworthiness of evaluations found in the informal apparatus may be vastly greater than any to be found in the formal apparatus; if a man evaluates a work on which he has labored for days or years, his evaluation has a greater prima facie claim to be taken seriously than does that of one who had, by the magnitude of his task, to evaluate quickly and superficially an enormous number of writings. Perhaps even more importantly, the things a man refers to in the course of serious discussion of a problem or topic are likely to be, not merely or primarily writings in which the same problem or topic is discussed, but writings that he has found useful in his own work: and these may be literally any writings at all.[2] What a man refers to is what he found good for his purposes, or strikingly bad for his purposes; he selects for mention some of the writings he has seen or used, and his selection is likely to be on the basis of principles which have no precise counterpart in the formal apparatus.

Let us turn again to the formal bibliographical apparatus. We may use an instrument successfully and yet not know our own power; for we may not know quite what we are doing, nor how much more we could do if we tried, nor what we could not do even if we tried. If we do not know the extent of the power that a particular instrument gives us, we shall not know what to make of our apparent failures, if there should be any, and

---

[2] Of course one is likely to refer also to writings in which the same problem or topic is treated, but even so one's references are likely to be selective, to what one thinks important rather than to everything one knows of that deals with the same problem or topic. Limiting oneself to the backward tracing of references is a foolish procedure if one's aim is to discover everything written on some subject, but not at all foolish if one's aim is to discover what has been thought significant enough to bother to mention.

Bibliographical Instruments 59

shall in fact be unable to distinguish failure from a sort of success. There is a distinction between not finding what we are looking for, and finding that what we are looking for is not there; the former is a failure, the latter a negative success. I do not discover the full extent of my power by reflecting on my positive successes, my occasional finding of what I seek; I must be able to recognize negative successes as well and distinguish them from failures to do what might have been done.

I cannot make the distinction accurately, however, without knowledge of the Specifications of the instrument, the rules according to which it was constructed. Even if I examine the contents of the instrument, item by item, I do not know what I can properly conclude about the items I find and, just as importantly, the items I do not find. My knowledge of the power given me by an instrument depends on the clarity of the rules according to which it was constructed, and on my knowledge of those rules. The less clear and exact the rules, or my knowledge of the rules, followed in the construction of the instrument, the less clear is my knowledge of the power given me by the instrument, and this means, the less able I am to predict what can and what cannot be done with the instrument. Evidently, knowledge of the Specifications is not by itself sufficient to allow such predictions; for I must know also whether, and how well, the Specifications have been followed, I must know the quality of the workmanship. But knowledge of the Specifications is nevertheless necessary, and indeed necessary for one who is concerned to evaluate workmanship as well as for one who simply wants to know what can be done with the instrument.

There are five sorts of elements in the specifications of most, if not all, bibliographical instruments. The first I shall call the *domain* of the instrument, the set of items from which the contents of the work, the items actually listed, are selected or drawn. The domain may be identical with the contents of the work, as in the case of a library catalog which lists every item the library possesses; ordinarily the domain will be larger than the set of works actually listed. If a bibliography claims to be complete, it claims in effect that the domain is the entire bibliographical universe, that there is nothing in that universe, except those listed, which would meet the requirements for inclusion in the bibliography. Since no one can any longer examine the entire bibliographical universe, it might appear that no instrument could have the universe as its true domain. But we need not demand that the domain be made coextensive with the set of works actually examined, or even available for examination; for there may be ways in which one can know without inspection that some set of items all fail to meet the requirements for inclusion, and items about which one knows this to be true, however one knows it, may be added to the domain. The domain, then, consists of the set of items about which the maker of the instrument is prepared to make a guarantee, the set of items from which he will guarantee to have drawn all that meet the requirements for inclusion. So a trustworthy bibliography tells us something about items not listed, as well as about the items listed: it tells us that a certain domain has been exhausted of one sort of material, and thus enlarges our power beyond the actual contents of the list. But it also indicates the limits of that power, if it tells us the extent of the domain, for it tells us what are the items, those outside the domain, about which we can draw no conclusion at all. Among the items outside the domain, in the "counter-domain," there may in fact be nothing that meets the requirements for inclusion, but no guarantee is made about that. Now it is very frequently impossible to determine the domain of an instrument; we may have no idea at all, or only very rough ideas, or we may have a fairly precise idea which is still "unhelpful," as in the case of domains specified as "library resources available in the immediate vicinity," when we have no idea what those are. But if we have no idea of the domains of bibliographical instruments, we have no idea of the extent of the power they give us.

The catalog of a library, a variety of bibliographical instrument, can have in a sense a double domain. The first is simply the total set of items possessed by the library; of these, many may not be listed in the catalog. But we may also consider the further domain, the set of all items considered for addition to the library collections. The value of a collection, and of the catalog of that collection, depend in part on the size of that further domain, as well as on the principles according to which selection from the further domain is made. If a systematic and deliberate attempt is made to make that further domain as large as possible, or to make it coextensive with some important segment of the whole bibliographical universe (the entire literature of geography or of geographical interest, for example), the catalog of the resulting collection is of vastly greater importance as a bibliographical instrument than it would be if the further domain were small or not systematically considered—provided, of course, that the wider domain is in fact carefully considered, and selection made according to some interesting principle.

All modern bibliographies are selective bibliographies, for no one now puts into a bibliography a description of every writing he is acquainted with; and the second thing we must know about an instrument, to estimate the power it gives us, is the principle, or principles, according to which items represented in it have been drawn from the domain. In the case of a self-proclaimed "selected bibliography," it is to be assumed that a double selection has taken place; from some set of items, those are chosen which meet some preliminary qualifications, for instance, being "about" a given subject, and then from that subset, a further selection is made, for instance, of those thought "reliable" or "standard." A bibliography will often indicate by its title the general nature of its selection principle, but a proper estimate of the power it gives requires a detailed statement of selection principles, so that we can predict the characteristics of the works not included as well as of those included. The vaguer the selection principles announced, the worse the position of the user of the work, for even if the selection was rigorously made according to precise canons, unless we can discover what those are, we do not know what predictions can safely be made about contents or domain. The selection principles tell us what claims we can make about the domain, but far too frequently the principles are not discoverable, and so we can make no claims.

Texts and works can be divided up and assembled in various ways, as can the units of the librarian's or publisher's universe, the books and pamphlets and issues of periodicals; and the third thing we must know about an instrument is how it is determined what is to count as a unit for listing and description. Most modern library catalogs give no separate listing to texts which happen not to be published as the entire contents of a physical volume; many such catalogs give no separate representation to texts occupying entire volumes, or even several volumes, if the volumes are part of a series published by a learned institution. One who does not understand this (and libraries do not loudly announce such matters) is almost certain to draw incorrect conclusions about his findings, and not-findings, in the catalogs he uses. Unless one understands the often quite complicated rules by which it is determined what is a "listable unit," one is likely to make the grossest errors in using an instrument. The size of the listable unit has a profound effect on the value of a bibliographical instrument; two instruments might have identical domains and selection principles but different rules for determining the size of unit to be separately represented, and that with the smaller unit is almost certain to be the more valuable instrument.

We must, further, know what information we can expect to find about an item, given that it will be represented as a unit. It is not enough to know what sorts of information we do on occasion find; we must also know what conclusions we can draw from the absence of a piece of information. We must be able to make negative inferences, to conclude that since it is not said of an item that it is so-and-so, therefore it is not so-and-so. Last, we must understand the frequently extraordinarily complex system of arrangement or organization: we must know where items of a given sort will be found, and what it means to find an item at a given place. This element of the Specifications deserves fairly elaborate discussion.

A bibliographical instrument might be rich in description of the items it lists and lacking completely in organization. If the items were listed in a purely random order, and if no provision were made for automatic or mechanical selection[3] of those having some feature in common (other than trivial features like being among the first hundred items listed), then and only then could we say that the instrument lacked organization completely. But if the items are sorted out into at least two groups in the list, or if provision is made by means of an index or similar device for identification of all the items fitting at least one description without scanning or reading through the entire list, then the instrument has a degree of organization. So a bibliography in which listings are divided into two groups, say, "Writings in English" and "Writings not in English" has a degree of organization, or, as we would say, has a very simple arrangement. So would a bibliography in which items were listed in random order but with an index indicating those in English; so would a stock of texts stored in the "memory" of an electronic device from which one could have produced all those to which some particular descriptive label had been attached. The practical effect of the application of an organizational scheme to a stock of items is that it allows the later immediate and direct identification of items that fit some description without the necessity of scanning all the descriptions of the items listed. Actual spatial collocation of listings is the ordinary way of doing this, but it should be clear that any index to a bibliographical instrument is part of its organizational scheme.[4]

Let us think of the organizational component of the Specifications as

---

[3] By "automatic or mechanical selection" I do not, of course, mean selection by a machine, but selection that can be done by people in a mechanical, "machine-like" way.

[4] "Organization," in my sense, is practically equivalent to what Jevons called "classification." "Under classification we may include all arrangements of objects or names, which we make for saving labour in the discovery of an object. Even alphabetical indices are real classifications."
—W. Stanley Jevons, *The Principles of Science* (London, 1905), p. 714. But I shall distinguish classification schemes, in which the available positions are themselves ordered on the basis

Bibliographical Instruments 63

consisting of the implicit or explicit specification of a number of *available positions*,[5] and of rules for the assignment of items to those positions. "Position" is meant here in a purely abstract sense, without spatial or temporal implications. Spatial applications and analogies can be made without harm, but if one uses analogies it is a good thing to use several, and we might also think of the available positions as resembling, not social positions but social *roles*. A classification scheme, one sort of organizational device, might consist of an enumeration of all the positions to which items were to be assigned, or it might, as do all the widely used library classification schemes, present in its schedules an enumeration of a basic set of positions plus instructions for the creation of new positions at need, thus implicitly specifying a definite set of available places, finite or infinite.

The schedules of a classification scheme might, on the other hand, enumerate no places at all, but rather list descriptive elements which, when combined in specified ways, would represent actually available places. Again, a list of subject headings or "descriptors" may likewise be an enumeration of all the available places or, as is true of the most widely used lists, may enumerate a basic set of places and give instructions for the addition of further places, by adding new terms to the list or by combining terms from the list to form new places. Organizational devices that neither enumerate places nor list elements to be combined in the specification of places also exist; rules of entry for personal names in an "author" list do not enumerate any positions nor list (except by way of example) any elements that would enter into the specification of a particular position, but rather give general rules for the construction of positions ("entries"), and implicitly specify an infinite number of positions.

---

of likeness and unlikeness of the things mentioned in describing the positions, or of the items assigned those positions, from organizational devices in which the order of the available positions is determined in other ways, e.g., by the alphabetical order of the names of the positions. See note 6 below.

[5] In a bibliographical instrument in process of growth, as a library catalog, many or even most of the available positions might be unoccupied. It might appear that the distinction between available/occupied and available/unoccupied had no point in the case of finished instruments, for only what has been done, not what might have been done, is of concern. But the distinction may even in such cases have a point. In a periodically published bibliography, the separate issues of which are finished though the whole is not, it may be imperative to note that, this year, there is nothing to record under such and such a description. In any finished bibliographical work, the bibliographer might do great service by including a "heading" and noting that, contrary to reasonable expectation, there was no literature that fell under that heading: that there was nothing to occupy that place. Quick "negative success" is only possible if one sees, not only what positions are occupied, but what further positions would have appeared, had there been anything to occupy them.

The available positions are simply abstract "locations," which might be identified simply by number or by other arbitrary marks. The *sense* of each position, that is, what we can infer about an item in virtue of its occupancy of a particular position, is given by the rules of application. In most organizational schemes the positions are identified not, or not only, by number or arbitrary marks, but by names or descriptive phrases drawn from ordinary language, names or phrases that incorporate or reflect the rule of application for particular positions, but do not give a complete interpretation of the position, do not completely specify the sense of the position. In a classified scheme rules of classification must also be given, no matter how elaborate the description in terms of which each position is identified; similarly for rules of assignment of subject headings in a subject list, and for rules of choice of "main" and "added" entries in an "author" list.

It is obvious enough that if one is confronted with an organizational scheme in which positions are identified merely by numbers, some rules of assignment or interpretation must be given in order that one understand the scheme. It is less obvious, when positions are identified by names or descriptions from ordinary language, that rules of assignment or interpretation are needed. But examples will make it clear enough. If we see a number of divisions of a bibliography each headed by a personal name, and we recognize the name, know whose name it is, we still do not know what will be contained in the divisions, whether writings by that person or about him, or even adversely critical writings about him: the distinguishing features of works assigned that position must be discovered by discovery of the rule assigning items to that position, a rule which will include reference to that person, or a general rule which will specify the relation between particular writings and the persons whose names identify particular places. If we see, in an alphabetical subject catalog, the heading ECONOMICS on a number of cards, we will think we know in part what the sense of the position is, simply because we know what economics is; but we do not yet know whether writings assigned that position are works of economics, that is, results of the pursuit of that branch of inquiry called "economics," or writings about the study of economics, or works that describe the range of phenomena that economists are interested in. For this we must know either a rule applying specifically to this position, or a general rule which fully interprets the position, a partial interpretation of which is given by the descriptive label. If we do not understand the ordinary sense of the label,

Bibliographical Instruments 65

we have no idea of the sense of the position; the word "horde" at the top of a card in an alphabetical subject catalog must be either meaningless or misleading to large numbers of people. And if the sense of the label is not the sense the words of the label have in ordinary speech, or in a particular man's own usage or "idiolect," then the label is, without rules of interpretation, completely misleading to one who sees it, and he has no sense (or no correct sense) of the position. But even if the words of the descriptive label have their customary senses, one who knows what those are still needs to know rules of assignment.[6]

Let us illustrate the need for knowledge of rules of assignment by an example that will also serve later purposes. Let us describe two different sorts of bibliographical instruments which we will suppose to have the same repertory of available positions and the same domains, selection principles, choice of unit, and principles of description. Let us imagine the repertory of positions to consist of a list of names and descriptive phrases (all of which we shall suppose ourselves to understand perfectly), which in ordinary speech are names and descriptions of any set of things we like, any collection of things that people might be interested in or curious about, any set of objects for investigation. The word "thing" is meant in its emptiest sense: not just physical objects, taking up space and time, but *anything*: objects, events, qualities, relations, real or imaginary, for instance the theory of palingenesis, the wrath of Achilles, the greatest positive integer, incubi and succubi, the routinization of charisma, witchcraft, space

---

[6] Differences in arrangement of the members of repertories of places is generally ignored in this discussion. Since we are discussing organization, and since "organization" is likely to be felt to mean primarily arrangement of positions, this omission may be seen as a great defect. But if a person knew what positions were available, and what the sense of each was, then ordering of positions according to a scheme of classification would do little for him except, perhaps, save an occasional bit of time. The saving of time is, while of enormous practical importance, of little theoretic interest. It must be recognized that the continual debate about the superiority of classified catalogs or of alphabetical subject catalogs is not simply a debate about the superiority of one method of arrangement of a single stock of available places or categories or terms, for the catalogs compared do not have identical stocks of places. If two catalogs were made that did have identical repertories of places, and if each were provided with appropriate auxiliary apparatus (an alphabetical index for the classified catalog, a classified conspectus of subject headings for the other), then, given identical principles of assignment to positions, the two catalogs would be perfectly equivalent in everything except, possibly, quickness of use. But if the repertories are not the same, or the assignment rules not the same, or the auxiliary apparatus not comparable (Cutter's proposed "synoptical table of subjects" never having been made for a large general subject catalog, no such catalog *is* comparable to a classified catalog with an alphabetical index), then the reasons for preference of one over the other form of catalog cannot be simply considerations of arrangement. For Cutter's proposal, see Charles A. Cutter, *Rules for a Dictionary Catalog*, 4th ed. (Washington, 1904), p. 80.

biology, whatever might be imagined or thought about.[7] The precise composition of the list is of no importance, nor are its terminology and arrangement.

Now let us imagine the list associated first with one, then with another, rule of application. The first rule specifies: Assign an item to a place N, just in case the description that identifies N is a closer description of the subject of the item than is any other description in the list. The second rule specifies: Assign an item to a place N, just in case the primary utility of the item lies in the help it would given to one engaged in the serious study of the thing mentioned by the descriptive label that identifies N. These rules are somewhat cumbersome, yet still not complicated enough; but I will suppose that the difference between them is in general clear enough. The first rule approximates[8] to a part of the rules according to which books seem to be classified and assigned subject headings in libraries, and the second is one example of a type of rule according to which writings would be assigned locations on the basis of their estimated utility or value for scholarship.

---

[7] The list is a list of *subjects*. It is not a list of *concepts*, but of things which we talk about by the use of words whose meaning can be identified with a concept. The thing referred to is not the meaning of the words by which we do the referring; following a long tradition, we distinguish sense or meaning on the one hand, and reference or denotation on the other hand. Failure to make the distinction produces nonsense of this sort: "This brings up the question as to the nature of the topic. A topic is a concept or particular nucleus of thought, usually expressed by a word, about which all aspects are gathered. Water, for example, is a concept which includes every aspect under which we may think of water. The concepts vary from general ones, such as Architecture, to more and more specific concepts, such as Cathedrals, Chancels, Altars, or even Altar Candles." It must be very frustrating to authors who, trying to write about the Queen of England or altar candles, find that they can only manage to write about the *concept* Queen of England or the *concept* Altar Candles. If they *do* succeed in writing about the Queen or about altar candles, they will have failed to write about the concept Queen of England or the concept Altar Candles, and so have failed to write about the corresponding topics. One can write about concepts, but most writings are not about concepts, but about other sorts of things, for instance, water, queens, candles. Julia Pettee, *Subject Headings* (New York, 1946), p. 57, is responsible for the previous quotation; others say the same sort of thing. I ignore the obvious fact that some of the terms in the list I give do not refer to anything "real"; for the fact that a man who writes about the luminiferous aether, thinking there is such a thing, is writing about what does not exist, does not make it true to say that he is writing about the *concept* of the luminiferous aether. Even a paranoiac who talks about his (in fact nonexistent) persecutors is not talking about the *concept* of his persecutors.

[8] Only approximates, and to only a part of the rules. Nothing is said here about "form" headings, for instance, nor about the cases of multiple assignments of subject headings. But I think it true that there is a rule, followed if not explicitly stated, to the effect that if there is a single subject heading that "adequately" describes *the* subject of a book, then only that single subject heading is to be assigned (a rule in effect at any rate in larger libraries). That there is not always such a single satisfactory heading necessitates further rules, but that is, as it were, a matter of unfortunate accident, and the single rule would be otherwise sufficient, and has in any case priority over all other rules.

Let us call the instrument constructed according to the first rule The Catalog, and that constructed according to the second rule The Bibliographical Encyclopedia. The first rule requires determination of *the subject* of a writing, the second requires estimation of what the writing is good for, or what "serious study" it would contribute most to. The two rules are plainly not equivalent; in the extreme case, we can imagine that each writing would be assigned different positions under the different rules, that no writing whose subject was X was of as great value to the study of X as it was to the study of Y, where X and Y are things described in the list. We would not expect this to occur frequently, but should expect it to occur occasionally, for the utility of a writing, if any, is by no means bound to lie in its contribution to the understanding of its subject. If I am seriously interested in the study of, say, concept formation among young children, I may get no help from the writings whose subject that is, but much help from writings whose subject is chimpanzees.

The essential difference between the two instruments does not disappear if we suppose the selection principles of both to have required evaluation of the writings selected. Even a bibliography of "best books" would be differently organized under the two rules, for under the first rule, assignment to location would be quite independent of any consideration of value; having decided that a work was worth listing, the decision about where to list it would be made solely on the basis of the subject of the writing. In practice the two sorts of rule are often found together; when attempting to find a unique place for an item in a classification scheme, in those common cases in which the item might equally well be put in two or three places, one will try to decide where the item will be the most useful, do the most good, and so apply a rule other than one requiring assignment on the basis of subject matter. But we can well enough imagine pure cases, in which only subject matter, or only expected utility, determine position.

The Catalog and The Bibliographical Encyclopedia have identical repertories of places, each identified by the same ordinary words and phrases with their ordinary meanings. Yet the senses of the places would, in the two instruments, be completely different, and a person unfamiliar with the rules of assignment or interpretation would totally misunderstand the nature of each. And so it is for all organized bibliographical instruments: unless we understand the rules of assignment, including the rules that interpret the descriptive labels if there are any, we cannot know what it means about an item that it is assigned a particular place, we cannot know what inferences we can draw about it and about the items which are *not* at its place. So we do not know what we are finding, and what we cannot expect to find, when we see an item at a place. Very simple organizational schemes may present few such problems of interpretation, but the complex schemes exemplified in great library catalogs and huge "subject" bibliographies are likely to be fully understood by no one, not even their designers. Almost nowhere do we find sufficient explicit statement of rules of assignment or interpretation to allow us to grasp fully the senses of the positions in a complex classification scheme or a large list of subject headings,[9] and it is not unreasonable to suppose that we do not find such explicit statement of rules because no such rules exist. But if no such rules exist, positions have no definite sense, and if we can discover no definite senses for positions, we cannot know the power, and the limits of the power, that bibliographical instruments give us. This may not matter very much to us; much of our use of such instruments is helter-skelter and not very serious, and we may be content with our positive successes and not care to distinguish negative successes from failures. If this is indeed true, bibliographers and catalogers waste much of their time, as they must at least occasionally suspect.

---

[9] The too infrequent "scope notes" found in lists of subject headings and classification schedules partially interpret particular positions, but do not fully interpret them, being no substitute for general rules of assignment.

Chapter V

SUBJECTS AND THE SENSE OF POSITION

There is an evident resemblance between the relation of The Catalog and The Bibliographical Encyclopedia on the one hand, and descriptive and exploitative control on the other hand. For the Encyclopedia is designed as an instrument of exploitative control, while The Catalog is, or seems, designed as an instrument of descriptive control. This does not mean that a work like The Catalog cannot include, in its descriptions, estimates of utilities, nor that a work like The Encyclopedia must be poor in description of the subjects of writings. But it does mean that the organizational bases of the two are such as to facilitate use for exploitative and descriptive purposes respectively. A work like The Catalog might be used in an attempt to discover suitable textual means to an end, as one like The Encyclopedia might be used in an attempt to discover items satisfying arbitrary nonevaluative descriptions; but it is plain enough that in either case one's success is likely to be less than it would be if more suitably organized instruments were used.[1]

An organizational scheme might choose any features at all of writings as the basis for assignment to position: size of copies, weight of copies, security classification, legal or social function, religious orientation. But of the familiar sorts of organizational scheme, those resembling that of The Catalog in assigning positions on the basis of subject matter are perhaps the most interesting and problematic. The instruments designed to provide what Shera[2] calls "content-accessibility" are without question the most difficult to make and the least generally satisfactory of bibliographical instruments. Jolley does not exaggerate in saying that the making of subject

---

[1] Goffman and Newill informally define "effectiveness," in relation to indexing systems, as "the measure of the system's ability to perform the task for which it was designed."—William Goffman and Vaun A. Newill, *Methodology for Test and Evaluation of Information Retrieval Systems*, Technical report no. 2, Comparative Systems Laboratory, Center for Documentation and Communication Research, School of Library Science, Western Reserve University (Cleveland, 1964), leaf 6; but they, and others who discuss the evaluation of such systems, appear frequently to suppose that the systems are *designed* to furnish materials relevant (in some sense, usually undefined) to particular requests. It seems to me much more plausible to suppose that most such systems are designed to furnish materials *on* specified topics, and that is a very different matter.

[2] Jesse H. Shera, *Documentation and the Organization of Knowledge* (London, 1966), p. 41; but his explanation of the term talks of subjects as *concepts*.

catalogs presents intractable difficulties,[3] and the same can be said of the making of classified catalogs and any considerable subject bibliography. No doubt subject catalogs and bibliographies can be made better than they generally are made, by taking greater pains and more thought; but not all the reasons for their unsatisfactoriness are reasons of poor workmanship or unsuitable or outmoded organizational schemes.

In the rule given earlier for the construction of what we called The Catalog, it was required that each item be assigned a single location, chosen on the basis of a prior determination of the subject of the writing. Not all instruments of "content-accessibility" require a single location, and not all require determination of the subject of each writing. But many do; and let us now ask whether there is not something in the notion of "*the* subject" of a writing which contributes to the intractability of the problems presented by subject catalogs and analogous instruments. If there is any obscurity in the notion of "*the* subject" of writings, it will infect any instrument whose rules of assignment resemble that of The Catalog. Now it seems to me that that notion is in fact a deeply obscure one, that the instruments in whose making that notion is employed are in important respects necessarily inscrutable, that in fact it is almost impossible, in such instruments, to arrive at an adequate sense of the positions to which writings are assigned.[4]

---

[3] L. Jolley, *The Principles of Cataloguing* (London, 1961), p. 98.

[4] "The concept of the subject of a book is not easy," says Jolley, and gives as a reason: "No subject exists as a completely separate entity. All subjects contain other subjects and are parts of larger subjects. The life of Queen Elizabeth is part of the history of England and *The Courtships of Queen Elizabeth* is part [sic! "describes part"] of the history of Elizabeth. It is also part of the history of France and Spain. All books deal with several subjects . . ." (op. cit., p. 99). But this is quite inconclusive, and no reason for thinking the subject of a book a concept more difficult than that of the author of a book. "One author is normally quite distinct from another author, and one title from another title" (loc. cit.); true, but any author is part of a family, and part of some society, and the author's history overlaps with the histories of his relatives and is included in the history of his society. A book about Elizabeth is a book about one whose private history is also part of the history of various countries, but a book *by* Elizabeth would have been a book *by* one whose private history was the same. If there is a difficulty about the concept of the subject of a book, it is not because it is hard to distinguish among subjects, for that is just the ordinary job of telling things apart, of distinguishing France from Spain, oil from vinegar, love from lust. Nor is it because subjects are "parts" of, or "included in," other subjects; authors are parts of, or included in, their families, which makes no trouble for the concept of authorship. Miss Pettee, *Subject Headings* (New York, 1946), p. 57, says that "It is in the nature of subject material that no topic is an entity in itself"; since she thinks topics to be concepts, this is all right if taken merely as a way of saying that concepts are not to be thought of as analogous to atoms or molecules. But if it is taken to mean that one cannot talk about a man without talking of his family, or about altar candles without also talking about all the other sorts of ecclesiastical furniture, it is rubbish, while if it means merely that everything is part of something, it is obvious and trivial.

Subjects and the Sense of Position

If a person tells us he is writing a book or paper, we may always ask him what he is writing about and will naturally expect that he will be able to tell us. One cannot write without writing about something or other and, further, one cannot write without knowing what one is writing, or trying to write, about. There may be ways of describing the results of writing or the process of writing which the writer himself would find surprising, but there must be some descriptions of what he is doing that he will not find surprising, and those must include descriptions of what thing or things he is writing about. And a reader of what another has written, if he understands the writing at all, must presumably share this knowledge; for how could he be said to understand the writing if he did not know what it was about? Further, what he knows, if he understands the writing at all, he can surely say; a man would deserve our suspicion if he claimed to understand a writing perfectly but was unable to tell us what it was about. The writer knows and can say what he is writing about, the reader who understands also knows and can say what the writing is about.

All this seems quite obvious, and not at all obscure. And so, in a way, it is. Let us see if we can go further. We seem willing enough in most cases to substitute, for the question "What are you writing about?," the question "What is the subject [or topic] on which you are writing?" To speak of the subject or topic of a writing seems to be merely another way of speaking of what the writing is about; the phrases "what a writing is about" and "the subject of a writing" seem perfectly equivalent. Behind the use of the definite article, *"the* subject," lies an apparently innocent assumption that there will be just one thing to mention in answer to the question "What is it about?"[5] And with that assumption goes another, that though there may be many ways of describing roughly or imprecisely what the writing is about, there will be just one perfectly precise description of what it is about. Of course the single perfectly precise description might be variously formulated; there may be different ways of putting the description, but these different ways will be mere alternatives among which one will choose freely, for they will be synonymous or nearly so. The perfectly precise description need not be brief, nor the one thing mentioned a simple thing; the precise description of what a paper is about might be "The Function of Follicular and Corpus Luteum Hormones in the Production of a Pre-

---

[5] The difficulty in the notion of "the subject" of a writing is to be located, as it were, in the word "the" rather than in the word "subject."

menstrual Endometrium in the Uterus of Castrate Monkeys (Macacus rhesus)."[6] But to suppose that there might be two equally precise yet non-synonymous and non-equivalent descriptions of what a writing is about seems to be the same as supposing that the writing is really two writings more or less cunningly joined together. If it is not about one thing, it is not one writing (though it may occupy all of one volume); and if there is not one perfectly precise description of what it is about, it is not about one thing.

Perhaps no one believes what is set out above about unique descriptions of single subjects; perhaps, for those inclined to believe it, it needs only to be set out to be seen to be incredible.[7] But if it is incredible, how can one account for the persistence of reference to "the subject" of a writing? Coates, for example, defines an "alphabetico-specific subject catalogue" as one in which the headings "state precisely the subject of each document, chapter, section, paragraph, or other literary unit chosen as the basis for indexing";[8] if he found it incredible that writings have single subjects, he would presumably not have given such a definition. Manuals of library practice are

---

[6] F. L. Hisaw et al., in *Anatomical Record*, 47 (1930), 300. There are those who would say that such a title is not in fact simply a description of the subject of the paper, but of its subjects and their "aspects." John Metcalfe, *Alphabetical Subject Indication of Information*, Rutgers Series on Systems for the Intellectual Organization of Information 3 (New Brunswick, N. J., 1965), pp. 30, 35–36, et passim, is one who appears to prefer to reserve the word "subject" to physical objects discussed, relegating everything else to "aspects" of "subjects," so that in the paper cited, the words "function" and "production" would not properly be construed as parts of the name of a subject. When one talks of "aspects," one is presumably talking of features or qualities of things, or ranges of facts about particular things; so the "legal and technological aspects of cheese" are presumably facts about the manufacture of, and laws relating to, cheese. But a body of law is a "thing" of a sort, which can be the subject of a writing, and manufacturing methods are another sort of "thing," equally a possible subject. There appears to be no good reason for saying that the only "things" that we can write and talk about are physical objects, nor any basis for a claim that some things cannot be considered as subjects but only as "aspects" of subjects. Nor is there any sufficient basis for the distinction, made by Sayers, between a subject and the "inner form" of the treatment of a subject. Of works on the philosophy of art, the theory of politics, the theory of science, Sayers says "each of these is distinctively on a subject: upon Science, Art and Politics respectively; but each is viewed in a special manner, from a special standpoint; in short, is in a special form," while in a history of science, the science "is the dominant idea of the book, and the history merely the method."—W. C. Berwick Sayers, *A Manual of Classification*, 3rd ed. rev. (London, 1955), p. 55. To write about the theory of science or the philosophy of politics is indeed to "view" science and politics "in a special manner," but it is equally proper, and rather more exact, to say that it is to "view" a special set of features of those things. The historian and the theorist of science look at, respectively, the course of events constituting the history of science and the logical structure of the results of scientific investigation. The move from "special standpoint" to "special form" is an illegitimate one.

[7] Of course no one thinks that all *books* have single subjects, for everyone knows there are such things as miscellaneous collections and anthologies.

[8] E. J. Coates, *Subject Catalogues* (London, 1960), p. 10.

full of references to "the subject" of a writing, and it can scarcely seem incredible to their authors that a writing that *is* one writing will have one subject. Those manuals are, however, curiously uninformative about how one goes about identifying the subject of a writing.[9] They recommend the examination of tables of contents, scanning of chapter headings, perusal of forewords and introductions. They will admit that "we cannot always determine what the subject is without some examination and thought; and even then, the chances of error are greater in this work than in any other known to us."[10] Coates, in his book on subject catalogs, describes the basic operation of subject cataloging as being essentially *summarization,* which he explains as "the abstraction of the overall idea embodied in the subject content of a given literary unit,"[11] and as "the art of reducing to a single idea the content of a piece of literature,"[12] which presumably implies that it is possible in general to reduce the content of a writing to a single idea, since subject catalogs do exist. "A subject heading might be described as an abstract which merely records the overall concept covered by the document in question."[13] Coates does not try to say how that reductive art is to be taught,[14] nor does he suggest ways of evaluating the products of the art; perhaps he thinks these the sorts of things which every intelligent person already knows. But even his brief account of the basic operation of sum-

---

[9] S. R. Ranganathan's discussions of what he calls "canalisation" might be expected to furnish the required instructions; but in fact they do not do so. Rather, they guide the classifier towards a particular sort of verbal *formulation* of a statement of the subject of a writing, one so corresponding to the structure of the classification system that "translation" of the verbal formulation into the "language of ordinal numbers" becomes mechanical. Ranganathan claims, *Prolegomena to Library Classification,* 2nd ed. (London, 1957), p. 229, that analytico-synthetic schemes of classification "enable him [the classifier] to determine the specific subject of the piece of writing exactly, however complex and involved it might be . . ."; with the aid of the prescribed analysis "in the idea plane," "the classifier can unerringly and almost mechanically break down the content of the piece of writing into its ultimates and spread them out into a spectrum" (p. 230). But the examples given are always of translating a verbal formulation into the classificatory language, never of discovering what the book is about. There is an elaborate discussion ostensibly devoted to procedures of determining the subject of a book in Ranganathan's *Library Classification: Fundamentals & Procedure, with 1008 Graded Examples & Exercises,* Madras Library Association Publication Series no. 12 (Madras, 1944); here the examples turn out to be simply instances of rewording the titles of books, but how one is to determine when this is required is not shown.
[10] Sayers, op. cit., p. 235.
[11] Coates, op. cit., p. 16.
[12] Coates, op. cit., p. 17.
[13] Coates, loc. cit.
[14] Coates, loc. cit.: "The teaching of the art of reducing to a single idea the content of a piece of literature is outside the scope of this book. It is allied to what is called 'comprehension' in language study and to abstracting in the technical sense."

marization seems defective, for it conceals the distinction between attempting to discern a central thesis or claim, which could be called a dominating "idea," and attempting to discover one thing which the whole writing could be said to be about. It is misleading to suggest that abstracting, the compression into a few sentences of a longer writing, and subject cataloging are simply longer and shorter varieties of the same process; one might manage to compress a summary of a writing into a single sentence, say, "Diamonds are a girl's best friend," but further than that one cannot go in the direction of summary, and indeed one might have gone that far without having at all decided on a proper subject heading, or being able, having arrived at the tightest summary, to decide. The dominant claim of a book, if it has one, need not be a claim *about* some item which the entire work would be said to be about.[15] Subject headings are not themselves summaries of writings; and if they do represent "overall concepts covered" or "overall ideas embodied" in writings, it is not necessarily by summarization of writings that appropriate subject headings are selected.

Let us go back to the seemingly unproblematical statements made earlier as to what a person knows who reads and understands a writing. Since he understands the writing, he must know and be able to say what it is about. But, understanding the writing, he must also understand each sentence of the writing (at least if his understanding is perfect), and if understanding requires "knowing what it's about," then he must know what each sentence is about. Further, if he were asked to say *how* he knows what the whole writing is about, what better basis could he cite than his knowledge of what each sentence is about? It is reasonable to suppose that the two sorts of knowledge are not independent, and that one might acquire the former on the basis of the latter.

---

[15] Monroe Beardsley's discussion of the interpretation of literature is useful here, *Aesthetics*, (New York, 1958), especially pp. 402–403. In addition to the subject or subjects of a poem, which are simply the things referred to by its words, he distinguishes *theme* and *thesis*. Asking about the theme of a poem is asking for some single concept or idea that can be seen to "connect" all the different things referred to, "something named by an abstract noun or phrase: the futility of war, the mutability of joy; heroism, inhumanity." Asking about the thesis is asking about doctrine or ideological content, or some general statement that the poem can be said to contain implicitly. So someone might say about a writing that its subject was such and such a war, its theme was human brutality, and its thesis was that the war resulted in a general lowering of standards of permissible behavior in wartime. No subject catalog would recognize either theme or thesis. On the distinction between abstracting and subject cataloging (or, more generally, indexing), see further Y. Bar-Hillel, "A Logician's Reaction to Recent Theorizing on Information Search Systems," *American Documentation*, 8 (1957), 103–113, reprinted in his *Language and Information* (Reading, Mass., 1964), pp. 313–329.

Subjects and the Sense of Position

Suppose we were to ask a man simply to *list* the things each sentence of a writing was about; it might be apparent, by examining the list, how one gets from a knowledge of what the individual sentences of a writing are about to a knowledge of what the writing is about. So we confront a man with a passage that begins:

> The Latins of Constantinople were on all sides encompassed and pressed: their sole hope, the last delay of their ruin, was in the division of their Greek and Bulgarian enemies; and of this hope they were deprived by the superior arms and policy of Vataces, emperor of Nice. From the Propontis to the rocky coast of Pamphylia, Asia was peaceful and prosperous under his reign; and the events of every campaign extended his influence in Europe.[16]

What shall he write down? Certainly something corresponding to the grammatical subject of each sentence, and indeed of each independent part of compound sentences. So the list must include "The Latins of Constantinople" and "Asia," but also "The sole hope of the Latins of Constantinople" (for "their sole hope" would not indicate whose hope), "The last delay of the ruin of the aforesaid Latins," and a suitable redescription of "the events of every campaign" that would indicate which campaigns were being talked of. But the list need not stop here, for having gone so far, one could not be said to be mistaken in adding to the list "Vataces," "Greeks," "Bulgarians," "the Propontis," "the coast of Pamphylia," and indeed anything named, mentioned, or referred to in the passage quoted. One must surely admit that, insofar as a sentence tells us something about items other than that corresponding to the grammatical subject of the sentence, it can with perfect propriety be said to be about those other items as well as being about the item corresponding to the grammatical subject. But what propriety allows, it does not also demand; if "the coast of Pamphylia" is not out of place in such a list, neither is its presence required. Nor does it appear that any particular verbal formulation could be required in the identification of an item named, mentioned, or referred to; there are presumably several ways of identifying the places Gibbon calls "the Propontis" and "Pamphylia," any of which would be admissible.

Let us imagine two experimental subjects faced with the same task, and responding by producing lists different in length and in composition. How might we proceed in attempting to evaluate the two lists? We might say

---
[16] The passage is from Gibbon, *Decline and Fall of the Roman Empire*, chap. 61. I do not think that choice of a passage from a less celebrated stylist would have led to different conclusions.

with confidence that omission of mention of an item corresponding to a grammatical subject was an error, that inconsistency in the treatment of analogous items was a mistake, that failure to write down words in the proper grammatical form to fit into the blank space in the frame sentence "The sentence is about ———" was an error, and that certain items on the list were definitely not anywhere named, mentioned, or referred to in the passage in question (the passage nowhere mentions Patagonia, for instance, and if a man claimed that "Pamphylia" meant Patagonia, he would clearly be mistaken). But, other than by pointing out mistakes of this last sort, could we have any reason for saying that one list was *too long*? It would be pointless to hope, by reference to the notions of naming, mentioning, and referring, to fix a definite "upper limit" to the length of lists produced under conditions like those imagined.[17] What might we say to one who suggested that the first sentence was about, inter alia, being encompassed, being pressed, and being deprived? or that the second was about, inter alia, peace and prosperity? If he claimed that verbs can well be taken to be names of actions, and that adjectives refer to conditions or states of affairs, we might dislike his semantic theory, but could scarcely convict him of a plain error of fact. Could he not go further and claim that there was a reference to time past (witness the verbs in the past tense), a mention of possession (witness "their sole hope"), and a reference to allness or totality (witness "every campaign")? For every concept employed, he could describe an item of some type, namely the, or some of the, instances of that concept, and claim a reference to or mention of the instances. The longest possible list of things a passage was about would be a list in which items corresponding to every concept employed in the passage, or to every meaningful item in the passage, were listed; but it is unlikely that anyone could say with exactitude precisely how many concepts, and which ones, were employed in even a quite simple passage. The supposition that one might get from a knowledge of what the separate sentences of a writing were about to a knowledge of what the writing as a whole was about is therefore complicated by the fact

---

[17] The concepts of naming and referring have been the subjects of very extensive discussion in the philosophical literature. Most of what is identifiable as the literature of (philosophical) semantics is concerned with notions like those of denoting, designating, referring, naming, mentioning. I shall mention only a few central writings: Bertrand Russell, "On Denoting," *Mind*, 14 (1905), 479–493, reprinted in Herbert Feigl and Wilfrid Sellars, eds., *Readings in Philosophical Analysis* (New York, 1949), pp. 103–115; P. F. Strawson, "On Referring," *Mind*, 59 (1950), 320–344, reprinted in Antony Flew, ed., *Essays in Conceptual Analysis* (London, 1956), pp. 21–52; W. V. O. Quine, *From A Logical Point of View* (Cambridge, Mass., 1953); and Quine, *Word and Object* (New York, 1960).

Subjects and the Sense of Position

that it is far from self-evident what, or how much, one must know in order to be said properly to know what a given sentence is about.[18]

Instead of attempting to decide which items a sentence is ("strictly speaking") about, which items are mentioned while not being items the sentence is about, and which items correspond to concepts employed without even being items mentioned or referred to, let us rather revise our instructions for the making of our lists: let us ask a person to write down, for the sentences given, a list of things named, mentioned, or referred to, and also

---

[18] There have been a few notable attempts by philosophers and logicians to straighten out the concept of aboutness, to say what it requires and what it does not require. One should refer to Carnap's discussion, *Logical Syntax of Language* (London, 1937), sect. 74, of what he called "pseudo-object-sentences"; as an example of sentences which assert something about the "*meaning, content,* or *sense* of sentences," Carnap gives "Yesterday's lecture was about Babylon." This sentence, he says, "appears to assert something about Babylon, since the name 'Babylon' occurs in it. In reality, however, [it] says nothing about the town Babylon, but merely something about yesterday's lecture and the word 'Babylon.'" Carnap is only incidentally concerned with the concept of being about, but clearly argues that any statement of what sentences or other linguistic units are about should properly be construed as statements about linguistic expressions only, not other sorts of things, so that "He is writing a book about Napoleon" contains a phrase which apparently, but not actually, refers to Napoleon. I think Carnap no longer holds the view that what appears to be mentioned when we *say* what a statement is about is not what it *is* about, or that what actually *is* mentioned is an expression or class of expressions.

A short article by Gilbert Ryle in *Analysis*, 1 (Nov. 1933), 10–12, entitled "'About,'" deserves mention. Ryle distinguishes three senses of "about," of which the third, "about-conversational," is of interest to us; an expression Q signifies what is the central topic of a conversation just in case all or most of the sentences occurring in the conversation contain that expression or a synonym or an indirect reference or allusion to what Q signifies, and there is no other expression (or referent) common to all the sentences. So what Q signifies or refers to is the topic by virtue of being of constant concern, constantly referred to or mentioned. This could at best be a *sufficient* condition for saying that what Q signified was the topic of a discourse, though I do not think it strictly even that. It could not be a necessary condition, as is evident on reflecting that a discussion of, say, a man's character might contain no occurrence of the word "character" or any equivalent expression. I do not suppose Ryle would now argue as he did in 1933.

The notion of being about is an eminent candidate for explication, replacement by precise, exact notions (see Chapter III, above). I am not presently concerned with proposals for reform, but rather with the consequences of the vagueness of ordinary language. So I shall merely mention two attempts at a formal explication of the concept of being about: Hilary Putnam's "Formalization of the Concept 'About,'" *Philosophy of Science*, 25 (1958), 125–130, and Nelson Goodman's "About," *Mind*, 70 (1961), 1–24. The latter has occasioned a reply and counter-reply: Nicholas Rescher, "A Note on 'About,'" *Mind*, 72 (1963), 268–270, and Alan Slomson, "Remarks on Rescher's Note on 'About,'" *Mind*, 75 (1966), 429–430. Goodman announced (op. cit., p. 22 fn.) the planning of a "memorandum concerning the bearing of the present paper upon problems of information retrieval," but I have not been able to discover such a memorandum, perhaps for lack of sufficient bibliographical control (descriptive) over "technical report literature," perhaps for lack of trying hard enough. In trying to understand ordinary operations with the concept of being about, I find more help in Peter F. Strawson's *Individuals* (London, 1959), especially pp. 142–153, than in the works just mentioned.

of concepts employed in addition to those employed in the naming, mentioning, and referring to things. Let us call such lists, Casts of Characters of sentences. People who produced quite different lists under the first instruction might be expected to produce more similar lists under this second instruction; one who denied, for instance, that possession and totality were referred to in the example above might easily agree that the concepts of possession and totality were employed. The longest list that one could be induced to produce, or accept from another, would be the list that in a certain way most fully reflected one's understanding of the passage; two people who accepted different lists for the same passage would be presumed to have different knowledge or opinions about the world or else to understand the passage in different ways, whether or not we could say that one of them misunderstood it. Now the amalgamation of lists for each sentence of a writing would constitute a Cast of Characters for the entire writing; and let us now put our problem as that of seeing how one could arrive at knowledge of what a writing as a whole was about on the basis of acceptance of a particular Cast of Characters for the whole.

Now it seems clear that knowledge of the subject of a writing does not arise automatically out of knowledge of the Cast of Characters of the writing. A person might read a list of names of presidents and not know or notice that the list was a list of presidents. He might trace the outlines of a picture of a cow and not notice that it was a picture of a cow. He might read a long description of the moral failings of another and not see that it was a description of moral failings. So it appears he might read any writing and, though understanding it a sentence at a time, and from one sentence to the next, fail to see what it was all about. Of course he must, if he is to grasp the writing as a whole, remember what he reads, for he could not say anything about the whole if he forgot each sentence utterly the instant he had finished reading the last word in it. But more than memory is required.

Let us try several different descriptions of how one gets from understanding the parts of a writing to knowing what the writing as a whole is about. The first we might call the Purposive way.[19] As we read a writing, and if we understand what we read, we come to see or realize what it is that the writer is trying to describe, report, narrate, prove, show, question, explain;

---

[19] Such rules of classification and subject cataloging as one can find will say things like "Consider the intent of the author," or "Consider the predominant purpose of the book." See, for instance, Sayers, op. cit., p. 235, or W. S. Merrill, *Code for Classifiers,* 2nd ed. (Chicago, 1939), p. 2.

we see what it is he is up to, what his object or aim or purpose is. His immediate object or aim, we must add, for we may also come to realize that he is describing this operation or trying to prove that point for some further purpose. What it is that we detect is an attempt on the author's part, successful or unsuccessful, to do a certain thing. Of course no very elaborate work of detection, or very remarkable insight, may be called for, since the writer may announce his purpose at the outset, and since most frequently, in works other than "imaginative" ones, he will give his work a name which can be taken to reflect, if not directly to describe, what he is attempting to do. A book may start out with a direct statement of purpose: "The object of this inquiry is to discover and develop Cook Wilson's view of the province of logic."[20] It may describe an attempt: "This book is the result of an attempt to make clear to myself what fifth-century Athens was really like."[21] Whether, or how well, the writer succeeds in his attempt or attains his object, is a question separable in principle from the question of what he is trying to do, though one can easily imagine cases in which the product was such a poor one that we would hesitate to call it a true attempt. Of course a man might misrepresent his purpose or lie about what he was in fact attempting to do; but it is less likely that he would do this about his immediate aim than about his further, his "ulterior" aim. In general we suppose that not only does a person know what he is trying to do, but is capable of giving, and willing to give, an honest statement of his aim; and knowing his aim, whether because he tells us or because we have detected or recognized it in his writing, we know what the writing is about. If he says he is trying to describe X, whatever it is, then normally we can say: X is the subject.

As human behavior is not in general single-minded or singly motivated, it will often be true that a writer aims at several things simultaneously, and that the different aims cannot be sorted out into a neat series of immediate, remote, ultimate aims. A man might aim at giving a satisfactory historical account of the eighteenth-century deist controversy in England, and also a critical and philosophical evaluation of the principal writers engaged in that controversy. If recognition of subjects were recognition of immediate aims, as many subjects would be recognized as there were recognizable immediate aims, and those just mentioned might be

---
[20] Richard Robinson, *The Province of Logic* (London, 1931), p. 1.
[21] Alfred Zimmern, *The Greek Commonwealth*, 4th ed. rev. (Oxford, 1924), p. 7 (preface to 1st ed.).

examples of simultaneous immediate aims, either of which might have been pursued independently of the other. But on the other hand, in the carrying out of a particular attempt, it may be or seem necessary to undertake subordinate tasks: in trying to give a satisfactory account of the deist controversy, it might seem necessary, as it did to Sir Leslie Stephen,[22] to "describe the general theological tendencies of the time"; and "in order to set forth intelligibly the ideas which shaped those tendencies," it might seem necessary to "trace their origin in the philosophy of the time," and in order to do that, it might be necessary to include an account of the contemporary style of philosophy.

Evidently the number and relationships of the secondary tasks undertaken may be large and complex. If we say that the subject of a writing is that which is aimed at, "primarily and immediately," the aim which governs the whole writing, the master plan pursued in all parts of the writing, then things done only because they are necessary preliminaries or means to the attainment of that immediate aim will not be accorded the status of subjects of the work. We will say that a work which discusses and is in that sense "about" "general theological tendencies of the time" can still have as its single subject the deist controversy, if the discussion of general tendencies is included only because it is thought necessary to the carrying out of the dominating aim or purpose. But if, on the other hand, we think that the discussion of general theological tendencies is itself an independent immediate aim, coordinate with that of giving an account of the deist controversy, then on the same principle we will say that the work has two subjects. So the number of subjects a work will be recognized to have depends on the number of independent aims that the writer can be recognized as pursuing (insofar as those aims are directed at distinguishable objects), and recognition of those requires an ability to see which of the things done or attempted in the writing are done only because necessary as means to an end, and which are done "for their own sake." But it is not clear how one does this. If the writer says "I only talk of X because I must, in order to give a clearer picture of Y," we will probably accept his claim. But suppose he tells us nothing of his aims: in that case, we must speculate,

---

[22] *English Thought in the Eighteenth Century*, 3rd ed. (London, 1927), p. viii (preface to 1st ed.). The Library of Congress assigned this work the single subject heading "Philosophy, English," though the heading "Deism" was available when the book was cataloged. Anyone who reads the book and attempts to formulate short descriptions of its content must be surprised that the Library of Congress could do no better than to say it was about English Philosophy.

and frequently it can be no more than speculation to claim that this or that is the "predominant" aim to which others are subordinate. It will frequently be that we will be unable to say what a book's subject is, or say it precisely, because we cannot discover purposes or choose among different possible descriptions of purpose.

It is difficult enough in any field of human behavior to discover a man's purposes by examining the results of his activity; and the difficulties must be much greater than ordinary in the case of those most complex products of human effort, writings. But there is further the difficulty that a person may in fact aim at nothing definite, that he may aim at different things at different times in the course of writing, that the "status" of his aims may change, what was ancillary becoming independent and even dominant, and so on through the list of vicissitudes of aims. Perhaps the most important is the first: one may have an aim, that is not directed at anything definite, an indefinite aim. Our descriptions of the subjects of writings may err as easily through over-specificity as through under-specificity, if they depend on our notions about aims and purposes. Even if a person announces a clear-cut aim, we may often wonder whether this is not the result of a post facto discovery or invention, the writing having in fact been guided by or directed to no clearly formulated goal but rather a vague and indefinite one. Serious attempts to discover the subjects of writings by appeal to purposes and aims cannot rest on simple authorial declaration, for those are as open to question as are any other actor's explanations of his own behavior. If the subject of a writing can be determined only by discovery of the writer's purposes and aims, we must as often be in doubt and disagreement about the subject of a writing as we are in doubt and disagreement about the explanation of writers' behavior, which is, if we are serious and even moderately skeptical, very often indeed.

However well we understand the parts of a writing, we may be unable to decide on the purpose that guided the composition of the writing, and so be unable to decide on its subject. But there are other ways of attempting to discover the subject of a writing. Let us proceed to describe a second way, one that we might call the "figure-ground" way. The Cast of Characters of a writing represents all the things the writing is in any way about, at least briefly. But not all of those characters occupy the same relative position or amount of space in the "picture" of the writing that gradually builds up in the reader's mind; an enormous number of the characters occupy small places in the background, against which stand out, more or less vividly, a few of the characters, grouped around some central figure. The central figure is *the* subject, and if two figures occupy equally prominent positions, they are the two coequal subjects. The central figure might indeed be a group of items rather than an individual item, but it will always be possible to distinguish the central item or group of items, which will stand out from the background of detail. A writing with a single prominent figure might concentrate on one after another of the parts or features of that figure, and some parts or features might be treated only sketchily or left in shadow. But insofar as the writing is satisfactorily constructed, it will be possible to pick out the dominant and the subordinate figures, and say which is more dominant or more subordinate than which.

This is a static analogy, of course; we can readily provide kinetic analogies. Reading a writing is like watching a moving picture: one object, in varying stages of a career or process, occupies the center of attention, other objects appearing briefly, still others forming a constant or recurrent background. Close-up shots of parts of the central object reinforce its dominance, but that dominance comes primarily from its being omnipresent or almost so, and as foreground rather than background. Two figures might be equally dominant, simultaneously or successively; in general, one will be able to discover a way of grouping distinct items so that there will be a single dominant figure.

In both the static and kinetic pictures, the impression of dominance is the important feature on which depends the identification of the subject of a writing; it is by reference to what "stands out" that we decide what is the subject of the writing, or by reference to what is "most emphasized."[23] But what seems to us to stand out depends on us as well as on the writing, on what we are ready to notice, what catches our interest, what absorbs our attention. The writer has some control over our sense of what dominates what, and the better the writer, the more control he has; but he does not have total control. The visual analogy may be misleading, for while there

---

[23] Cf. Sayers, op. cit., p. 47: "A classification of books does not attempt to arrange them by all their subjects, but only by the predominating, or most convenient, subject in each." This suggests that Sayers does not think writings in general have unique subjects; but contrast the implication of uniqueness in the quotation given above at note 10, and what is said on p. 238 of the work cited. We might paraphrase the sentence just quoted thus: "A classification of books does not attempt to arrange them by all the things they discuss or mention, but only by the things that predominate or are most usefully singled out." Of the various "subjects," that is, things discussed, the one that predominates is nominated as The Subject.

can be no argument about an object's occupying the center of the "picture space," there can be argument about an object's being the center of attention or the most emphatically mentioned item in a writing; the omnipresent figure may seem to one just a constant "background" item, but to another the single impressive thing in the writing. Dominance is not simple omnipresence; what we recognize as dominant is what captures or dominates our attention, but we cannot expect that everyone's attention will be dominated by the same things.

Such analogical talk is unsatisfactory enough, though it does correspond to "reality," for we do frequently enough support our claims about what the subject of a book is by reference to what seems most emphasized or most to stand out. But we may try a third, more "objective" way of describing how we identify the subjects of writings. Let us think of simply counting references to items. If we see the name "Hobbes" recurring again and again, and no other name frequently recurring, if we count not only occurrences of the names "Hobbes" and "Thomas Hobbes" and "Thomas" but all pronouns and descriptive phrases by which Hobbes is referred to (e.g., all the occurrences of 'him" when the him meant is Hobbes), and proceed likewise for all other referring phrases in the writing, with the result that references to Hobbes vastly outnumber references to anything else at all, is this not a good reason for saying that Hobbes is the subject of the writing?[24] This is in part the "objective correlate" of the impression of dominance, for one way of making an item seem to dominate a writing is by referring to it constantly. But it is clearly only a partial correlate, for the impression of dominance depends also on the sorts of things said about an item, and the style of the saying. The constantly-referred-to item might be merely a background item, as a history of happenings in Petrograd might mention Petrograd constantly while the action was described in terms of a succession of different persons and their various doings. Mere numerical predominance of references cannot uniquely determine a subject; this obvious truth is reinforced by the reflection that one can always rewrite a text in such a way as to reduce the number of references to any item and increase the number of references to any other without materially altering the general sense of the writing or even, if one were skillful enough, changing the balance of impressions of dominance and subordination.

The counting of references can take place in a more complex fashion and

---

[24] This is akin to Ryle's "about-conversational" (above, note 18).

indeed must if it is to yield intuitively acceptable results. One can group items referred to in various ways, and if a preponderance of references in a writing can be construed as references to parts or segments or features or members of a complex object or group, then all the references can be reconstrued as indirect references to that object or group, and in this way a single object may be picked out as the best candidate for the position of subject.[25] Consider a particularly simple sort of case, that of a biographical writing. A person's life can be divided into temporal segments (the first five years, the next five, and so on) and into strands (professional life, sexual life, and so on); the events of a life can be grouped variously into segments and strands picked out in a multitude of ways. It is easily seen that a writing said to be on the subject of the political career of a certain man might contain no occurrence of the words "political career" or any equivalent expression, and that there might be no reference to that strand of his life at all. All the references might be to particular events which we take as events *in* the political career, and so say that the writing is about the political career. Or the only object of constant reference was the man himself; to describe him as being the subject might still be hopelessly imprecise, but to describe his political career as the subject requires our grouping references or, more generally, grouping the Cast of Characters according to a principle which we ourselves supply. To mention the single object of constant reference may not be to identify the subject; to identify the subject may be to mention something which is not one member of the Cast of Characters at all.

---

[25] If we allow ourselves to say that a reference to what is part of another thing is an indirect reference to that other thing, and that (as seems natural enough, given the first sort of indirect reference) a reference to a thing is an indirect reference to any part of that thing, the consequence will follow that any statement about anything is indirectly a statement about the totality of things and that any statement about any part of the universe containing my left thumb is indirectly a statement about my left thumb, which seems silly. Since the references are indirect, perhaps the air of paradox can be borne. If we allow doubly indirect references, so that an indirect reference to a thing is an indirect reference to its parts and to what it is part of, then a reference to anything is an indirect reference to my left thumb, which is going too far. Goodman finds a similar paradox (op. cit.) by supposing that a statement about any thing is a statement about whatever that thing is part of or contained in, and also about whatever that thing contains or has as parts; so a statement about Florida is a statement about Maine, since Florida is contained in the United States and the United States contains Maine. Goodman tries to avoid the paradox that to talk about anything whatever is to talk about everything else by distinguishing "absolute" from "relative" aboutness, similar to our direct and indirect reference, though he is precise where we are intentionally vague. Without the notion of indirect reference, I think that we can get nowhere in counting up references in our search for the subject; but with that notion, we seem to get too far.

Subjects and the Sense of Position

The method of identifying subjects by counting references is a hopeless one unless we allow ourselves to count indirect references, to group items referred to and consider a reference to a member of the group to be an indirect reference to the group. But if we do allow ourselves to do this, it is quickly apparent that no unique results can be expected; for there are many possible ways of grouping any set of items referred to, and any Cast of Characters. One immediate result is that every writing has a unique subject determined by the Cast of Characters: a writing is about its Cast of Characters, that cast is its subject.[26] This is by no means an unwelcome result, in my view; there is nothing wrong with answering the question "What is this writing about?" by giving the Cast of Characters. But Casts of Characters are groups without names; there is no recognized, established word or phrase applying just to the Cast of Characters of any writing. The cast is an ad hoc group, unique to a particular writing. The groups we will recognize will be those for which we already have names, groups assembled on the basis of some concept we already possess, groups that seem to us "natural." Because we have the concept of a political career, and the concept of a private life, we can recognize the events described in a biography as all belonging to the categories of events in a political career, or events in a private life, or as mostly belonging to those categories. But there may well be other ways of grouping things referred to that seem equally "natural" to those who have, or think of employing, different concepts. We may try to discover a single subject (other than the whole Cast of Characters) by counting references and indirect references; but the results will depend heavily on our ingenuity in finding ways of assembling groups, on our stock of available notions, on our ability to unify a writing by discovering or inventing a concept which all or much of the writing can be taken as exemplifying in one way or another.[27]

---

[26] If, that is, we can agree on the composition of the Cast of Characters. We might agree that each writing had a unique Cast of Characters but be far from agreement on its exact composition. But is it at all certain that a given writing must employ some definite number of concepts? Must concepts be countable?

[27] To limit the use of indirect references and cut the possible number of groupings of Casts of Characters to manageable size, we might invoke the notion of *comprehensiveness*. Cutter in *Rules for a' Dictionary Catalog*, 4th ed. (Washington, 1904), p. 16, speaks of classification by subject as being, in one sense, "bringing together books which treat of the same subject specifically. *That is,* books which each treat of the whole of the subject and not of a part only." (My italics.) So we might say: We may recognize X as the subject of a writing, even though X is not mentioned, if *all* of the parts of X are mentioned. (We could then weaken this to read "if practically all of the parts . . . are mentioned.") So a book might be about California either

The countings and groupings imagined do correspond to an ingredient of many actual decisions about subjects; the claim of an item X to be regarded as the subject will be supported by citing the "great amount that is said about it," "the amount of space devoted to it," and the like. It seems plausible to measure the amount said about an item X in terms of the number of references to X (not merely the number of occurrences of the term X), since any statement containing a reference to X can be construed as "saying something about X," directly or indirectly. What is said may not amount to much, may not give much "information," but how often an item is mentioned, or a concept employed, is obviously a consideration relevant to a decision about what the subject is, and may in some cases be the only one.

There is still another way of describing what people do in identifying subjects: this might be called the appeal to unity, or to rules of selection and rejection. (I shall combine what might well be separated.) Let us consider this account of what a subject is, by prominent scholars: "... your subject is defined by *that group of associated facts and ideas which, when clearly presented in a prescribed amount of space, leave no questions unanswered* WITHIN *the presentation, even though many questions could be asked* OUTSIDE *it.*"[28] A writer starts with some idea of what he is going to write about; the discovery of the "true whittled-down subject" ends only with the completion of the work. For in the process of writing, he is forced to select and reject among things that might be said, that somehow bear on or are related to the kernel or initial notion. "There has to be unity and

---

because California was constantly referred to, or because practically all the parts of California were referred to, and nothing else was constantly referred to. But this rule would not give generally acceptable results; a book which referred to Northern California once and to each of the counties of Southern California hundreds of times would by this rule count as being about California, or indeed about the United States, if it, or each of the other states, was mentioned at least once. In any case there are innumerable numbers of ways of dividing any thing up into "parts," and we would be hard put to say in general when "all parts" of a complex thing had been mentioned. The notion of "treating the whole of a subject" is itself an incorrigibly vague one: in a sense it is impossible to treat the whole of a subject, for that might be taken to mean saying all that could be said about the subject. A biography of a man which omitted reference to his first twenty years of life would be said not to have treated "the whole of the subject," yet one which omitted reference to his psycho-sexual development in the first five years of life would not on that account alone be considered not to have treated "the whole of the subject," even though that is as good a strand of a person's history as any other. Our notions of what is required for completeness are both exceedingly vague and subject to radical change; what a history required for completeness in the eighteenth century and what a history now requires are very different things.

[28] Jacques Barzun and Henry F. Graff, *The Modern Researcher* (New York, 1957), p. 20.

completeness"; what he says must all hang together, he must say enough but not too much. As he goes on, he becomes more and more assured of what belongs and what does not belong in the writing, of what is required and what is dispensable, what is "necessary" to the completeness of the writing and what is unnecessary. This can be seen as the gradual formulation of rules of selection and rejection, and that gradual formulation is exactly the same as the gradual realization of what one's "true whittled-down subject" is.

That writings should be unified, coherent and in some sense complete is not to be argued; it is an excellent reason for criticizing a writing that one cannot see the connections among its parts, that it leaves loose ends, that it does not answer the questions it raises. It is also evident that not all writings attain this ideal, and it is a glaring defect of the above account of what a subject is, that it incorporates the ideal in the definition. For it follows from the above account that a work may lack a subject simply because it raises questions it leaves unanswered. But the account is a useful one nevertheless. First, the "group of associated facts and ideas" bears a close resemblance to a description of the Cast of Characters (not an exact one, to be sure, for the Cast includes no "facts," only items mentioned and concepts employed in the stating of facts); and this account reinforces the conviction that describing the subject of a writing must be, in one aspect, describing that group of "associated facts and ideas" or, in our terms, describing the whole Cast of Characters, not just picking out the biggest member. But second, the account reminds us that identifying the subject of a writing is also attempting to discover a way of unifying the Cast of Characters, and of accounting for the presence of the different members. One picks out one member, or forms a group of members, not just because it is the biggest or most frequently mentioned, but because it is that by reference to which the presence of the rest can be explained, it provides a sufficient reason for their being mentioned.

It is frequently the case that a gross and imprecise description of what a writing is about is immediately available: the writing is somehow about the Russian Revolution, or has something to do with medieval technology. The attempt to say *exactly* what the subject is, is best seen as an attempt to discover some rule of selection or rejection which will at once allow a more precise description of the subject, and an explanation of the presence of discussions of things other than the thing identified as subject: a rule to the effect of, say, "Put in only what directly relates to explaining the fall of Kerensky," or "Put in only what will illustrate best the effect of medieval technology on medieval society." If we can find such an imagined rule (which we need not suppose to have been consciously formulated by the writer), which does function to explain the presence of most if not all of the Cast of Characters and at the same time allows us to pick out one precisely described item by reference to which the others are explained, we shall feel we understand how the writing hangs together, and what its subject really is. But it is too evident that this effort may result in a piece of artistry on our part rather than on the part of the writer; discovering how the writing hangs together may be discovery of one out of several possible ways in which we can make it seem reasonably unified, coherent and complete, ways whose success or failure could be judged only on predominantly aesthetic grounds.

We have roughly described several different ways of arriving at descriptions of the subjects of writings. There is no reason to think that following the different ways would always lead to the same result. We can easily imagine that the subject of a writing would be differently described according as one relied on the identification of the writer's aims, on the weighing of relative dominance and subordination of different elements in the picture one formed of the writing, on the grouping and counting of references or employments of concepts, or on the inventing or guessing at rules of selection. Yet none of these procedures seems inappropriate to the task; each seems to have a reasonable claim to being *a* way of picking out the subject of a writing. If they gave the same result, as presumably they often would, there would be no doubt that *the* subject had been identified.

But when they gave different results, as it is almost beyond doubt they would sometimes do, how could the differences be reconciled? If two or three gave the same result and the others gave different results, we would probably choose the majority result, though it is hard to see how we would justify such a preference for majority rule. And there is no apparent "natural" order of priority among the different methods. We are not obliged to give precedence to a writer's own statement of aims, for it is well known that men frequently fail to do what they say they mean to do. The tests of reference-counting and impressions of predominance may offset each other: that most space is devoted to one item or group of items does not destroy the contention that something to which less space is devoted is the dominant item, that the "emphasis" is on it. To discover or invent an organizing principle for the writing, in terms of which it appears unified and coherent and complete, is not to do something that is obviously a better way of discovering the true subject than the other ways. So a single reader, trying by different means to arrive at a precise statement of the subject of a writing, might find himself with not one but three or four different statements. And if several readers tried the several methods, we should not be surprised if the same method gave different results when used by different people. Estimates of dominance, hypotheses about intentions, ways of grouping the items mentioned, notions of unity, all of these are too clearly matters on which equally sensible and perspicacious men will disagree. And if they do disagree, who is to decide among them?

The notion of the subject of a writing is indeterminate, in the following respect: there may be cases in which it is impossible in principle to decide which of two different and equally precise descriptions is a description of the subject of a writing, or if the writing has two subjects rather than one. A writing might be such that there were equally good grounds for saying it had as its subject the commercial adventures of some imperialist power, with some supporting detail on military adventures, and for saying that the subject was the military adventures, with supporting detail on commercial adventures, or for saying that each of these was an independent and equal subject of the writing, that it had not one but two subjects. Of two descriptions, which are not descriptions of the same thing, it may be impossible to say whether both describe subjects of the work, or whether only one describes the subject; and of two descriptions, one of which is a description of only a part of what the other describes, it may be impossible to say which accurately describes the subject. The difficulty is not one that will be avoided in practice simply by lifting the requirement of single location for single items, and allowing assignment to as many places as are required in order to represent the various subjects of the writing; for how many are required is precisely what may be undecidable in principle. The vaguer and more general our statement of the subject of a writing, the less likely it is to be open to question; the more exact and precise we try to be, the more likely it is that several equally exact descriptions, of different things or larger and smaller segments of one thing, will be formulable, among which we cannot choose except arbitrarily.

Any actual physical object is, as the old philosophers would have said, "determinate in every respect"; whether we can decide on its actual shape and size and weight and color, it must have some definite shape and size and so on, at any moment. There are no doubt limits to the precision of measurement and description possible to us, but there must be some descriptions which are the exactly correct descriptions of its various characteristics, even if we cannot, because of physical limitations, tell which ones those are. Things are what they are; our descriptions may be vague and imprecise and indefinite, but there can be no vagueness or indefiniteness about the things themselves. Now we have an inclination to say that what is true of things must be true of writings "about" things; a writing must have a definite subject, and there must be some description of the subject that is absolutely precise and accurate, all other descriptions being imprecise or inaccurate. It is this inclination which must, I think, be resisted; of course we can always formulate descriptions which are obviously and definitely *not* descriptions of what a writing is about, but we cannot expect to find one absolutely precise description of one thing which is *the* description of *the* subject, all others being mere approximations to that one description, or being descriptions of what is not the subject. The uniqueness implied in our constant talk of *the* subject is non-existent.

The consequences of this indeterminacy for organizational schemes based on identification of the subject of a writing should be clear. The sense of a position in an organizational scheme is given by the rules of assignment and by what we can deduce from those rules. When position is assigned on the basis of identification of the subject and selection of the most closely fitting position, whatever sense we have of positions depends on what we know about how it is decided what the subject of a writing is, hence what it means to say of a writing that its subject is this or that. And what can we claim to know of those things? The ways described above are only possible ways; we do not know how people actually proceed. If position is assigned on the basis of identification of some determinate feature of writings, we can know that items at a position will share features in common, and in some respect differ from items located elsewhere. But what can we predict about what items at a position will have in common, that will distinguish them from items everywhere else, if position is assigned on the basis of identification of subject? Of the items at other positions, some might have been assigned this position if a different method had been employed of identifying subjects; items at other positions may resemble some of the items at this position more closely than the items at this

Subjects and the Sense of Position 91

position resemble each other, and this not because of mistake on the part of the locator, but because of the indeterminacy of the notion of the subject of a writing. No single feature, and no cluster of features, set off the writings at one position from those at all other positions; the rules of assignment prescribe nothing definite, and no confident predictions can be made about what will be found in the writings at a given place. So the place has no definite sense.[29]

Those who recall their own past successes in identifying the subjects of writings and in classifying and assigning subject headings are likely to doubt the force of the above claims. They had no trouble, in most cases, and so how can it be true that positions in a subject organizational scheme have no definite sense? But their successes are not to the point; catalogers and bibliographers do not have time to brood over alternative possibilities, nor do they need, in most cases, to attempt a very precise description of subjects. It is their job to locate items quickly, and the organizational schemes they use are mostly too coarse to allow or require the making of fine distinctions. They find a location which satisfies them, and count this a success. But the user of their work finds himself unable to understand the product; or, mistakenly, supposes he understands when he does not. For years, Cutter's statement[30] that one of the objects of the "dictionary catalog"

---

[29] This is not to say the place has *no* sense. Nor is it to say anything at all about the similarities and dissimilarities among writings that happen in fact to be found at a particular place or selection of places; what may be discovered a posteriori is not the point at issue. Rather, it is to say: there is no single feature, nor any combination or disjunction of features, that we can specify in advance in a general statement of this sort: "All the writings in this collection that have feature F must, if the Specifications have been correctly followed, be at place N." All we can say, in advance of actual examination of texts, is: "At place N are all the writings which our methods, applied by our workers, assigned to that place," and this does not tell us much. The indeterminacy of the subject seems to furnish further support for Jevons' famous remark that "Classification by subjects would be an exceedingly useful method if it were practicable, but experience shows it to be a logical absurdity."—W. Stanley Jevons, *The Principles of Science* (London, 1905), p. 715. No doubt he had other reasons in mind.

[30] Cutter, op. cit., p. 12. Cf. Jolley, op. cit., p. 100: "It is usually stated that the object of the subject catalogue is to show what books there are in the library on a particular subject. 'On' is the ambiguity which destroys the neatness of this definition. Does it mean 'devoted wholly to' or 'giving substantial information about'? In either case it can be stated with certainty that no subject catalogue has ever answered this question [? "achieved either aim"] with more than a partial success." But those who are quite clear that Cutter's objective is never attained are frequently not so clear on why it is not. See J. Kaiser, *Systematic Indexing* (London, 1911), para. 255: "Dewey says: 'Since each subject has a definite number, it follows that all books on any subject must stand together' (on the shelves). That sounds very businesslike, but a moment's reflection will show that it is merely shutting one's eyes to the real difficulty. Because we give a book a definite number it does *not* follow that the book has a definite subject. If every book or even the majority of books were confined or could be confined to one definite subject, then we could agree with him. But books do treat of more than one subject, that is

of a library was "to show what the library has ... on a given subject" has been repeated, without explanation, as if it were obvious what "being on a given subject" meant. For as many years it has been pointed out that, under a given topical heading in a catalog, only a fraction of the material in the library's collection on the topic named is likely to be found listed. If it had been in fact the aim to collect, under a given heading, references to all discussions of the topic named, subject catalogs would always have been seen to be ludicrous failures. But evidently "on a given subject" contains a quasi-technical term which is nowhere explained; to the librarian, "being on a given subject" *means* "being the sort of writing which our methods of assigning single locations assign to the position with such and such a name." When a lay person asks for books on the subject of X, he does not mean the phrase "on the subject of" as a librarian or cataloger means it; he means something both vaguer and of much wider application, roughly equivalent to "containing a fair bit of talk about" or "discussing." He must very frequently be surprised by what he finds, and what he does not find, in subject catalogs or classified catalogs under the description of that in which he is interested. But there is, if the preceding account is even roughly correct, no easy way of educating him so as to forestall surprise; for nothing definite *can* be expected of the things found at any given position.[31]

---

the real difficulty. . . . Two books treating of widely different subjects primarily may both include the same secondary subject, they will be separated by his classification in spite of what he says, for you cannot give the same book two places on the shelves." Surely Dewey did not suppose that a book on, say, Napoleon mentions no one but Napoleon, but rather that, for any writing, there will be one thing that it treats *primarily*. That is all, in any case, that Dewey need have claimed.

[31] It is tempting to think that, if only the words we used to describe the contents of writings were clear and precise in meaning, the intractable difficulties of content-accessibility would vanish or be largely overcome. It is true that the words we use to describe the contents of writings are imprecise and vague and ambiguous, and that different people use words in different ways, and that these facts account in part for the troubles of subject catalogs and bibliographies. It is true that "Because there is this lack of precision in the fundamental units which we are using to index our collections, we cannot expect to achieve a greater level of precision in our analysis than we have in the tools or words which we use in making that analysis."— C. D. Gull, "Seven Years of Work on the Organization of Materials in the Special Library," *American Documentation*, 7 (1956), 321. But no sharpness of tools would eliminate difficulty; greater sharpness might increase difficulty. For instance, I know more or less clearly what hostility is, that is, the word "hostility" has a fairly sharp meaning for me, but far from a perfectly sharp and precise meaning. Now if I were to supply myself with an exactly defined concept, got by explication of my imprecise notion, I might find that I could never use the new concept in describing any actual piece of writing; the concept might be too sharp ever to find application. There would be instances of hostility (in the new sense) that I could recognize, but no instances of writings on hostility that I could recognize, for no one would have written on hostility (as I now would understand it). If people write on what are for them ill-defined phenomena, a correct description of their subjects must reflect the ill-definedness.

CHAPTER VI

INDEXING, COUPLING, HUNTING

IT IS OBVIOUS to everyone that the value of a writing is not in general in direct proportion to its length, that a brief paragraph in one writing may be worth more than whole treatises. A perennial concern of bibliographers is to make available "the individual thoughts that outweigh whole books, periodical articles, or chapters," as Georg Schneider put it.[1] But how is this to be done? How can we ever ensure that a man will be able to discover the "individual thoughts" that will be of greatest value to him? Bibliographical instruments of the sort discussed above are plainly not efficient for the purpose, a fact we know without the need of elaborate experimentation. But what sort of bibliographical instrument would be appropriate?

If we wish to reveal the contents of a field of writings very fully, we may pursue either of two quite different tactics. We can divide the writings into very small parts, and assign each part a single location in a repertory of positions large enough to allow us to make very fine discriminations of subject matter, to find for each small part a place corresponding exactly to our description of the subject of the part. Or we can select larger units of writings and assign each unit as many positions as we like in the same exhaustive repertory.[2] If we pursue the first, the problems of identification of subject rehearsed above will be repeated and perhaps exacerbated, for we cannot hope that it will be easy to identify unique topics for individual chapters or paragraphs of a writing. A well-written paragraph may, according to our canons of style, have a topic-sentence and a "leading idea," but

---

[1] Georg Schneider, *Handbuch der Bibliographie* (Leipzig, 1923), p. 51: "... machte sie doch vielleicht Einzelgedanken nutzbar, die ganze Bücher, Zeitschriftenartikel und Kapitel aufwögen."

[2] The difference is that between, for instance, identifying a single subject in each of a book's ten chapters, and identifying things discussed, whether all at once or in scattered fragments; in the former case, anything not the subject of one of the linear units of text would go unrecognized; in the latter case, nothing need go unrecognized. The distinction requires to be stated rather differently in the case of "coordinate indexing" systems, in which each available position is associated with a "unit concept" (not necessarily expressed by a single word). In such systems, representing a "single subject" may require assignment to many positions, which taken or "read" together (with or without "role indicators" giving syntactical information and "links" indicating that these positions *are* to be taken or read together in this case) are the equivalent of what in other systems would be a single position. With this qualification, I think the distinction applies generally. On these indexing systems, see John C. Costello, Jr., *Coordinate Indexing*, Rutgers Series on Systems for the Intellectual Organization of Information, 7 (New Brunswick, N.J., 1966).

by no means all paragraphs are well written.[3] But rather than continuing the discussion of determination of the subject of a stretch of writing, let us consider the alternative procedure, which is to abandon the attempt to identify unique subjects of given pieces of writing, and to assign a writing, of any length, to as many positions as we like or can afford. This I shall speak of as *indexing,* for while there is no sharp distinction to be made between conventional classification and subject-cataloging on the one hand, and indexing on the other, still the more descriptions we allow ourselves to make of the contents of a writing, the more detail is revealed, the more likely it is that our activity will be called "indexing" and the result an "index."[4]

Let us once again employ the notion of the Cast of Characters of a writing. A list of the Cast of Characters of a writing, with indication of where in the writing each one appeared and for how long, would in fact constitute an index in the most conventional sense, though a much more detailed one than is customary. Not even such a device could be considered as *the* ultimate, final index of a writing, of course; for there is, as previously argued, no inevitable uniqueness in the product of the activity of drawing up Casts of Characters. But a carefully drawn up Cast is much more likely than are conventional indexes to exhibit that "rigid attention to the merest detail" which is said to be required in certain sorts of indexes, and to attain the "highest level of exhaustivity."[5] Since the Cast includes concepts em-

---

[3] About paragraphs see, for instance, John Halverson and Mason Cooley, *Principles of Writing* (New York, 1965), p. 232: "A well developed paragraph is very much like an essay in miniature, with a clearly defined thesis (a topic sentence) backed by supporting material that is arranged in a definite pattern." But not all paragraphs are good ones. It is common to find the paragraph explained as containing "the full development of a single idea," which is ridiculous. The paragraph is a device of punctuation. See Herbert Read, *English Prose Style* (Boston, 1952), pp. 52–54 et ff.

[4] The *negative* distinction between a catalog and an index with the same repertory of positions is simply that the rules of assignment of the former, but not of the latter, would require an initial identification of the (unique) subject of each item (with the possible result that the item was decided to have more than one subject). There is no limit to the number of positive distinctions. According to one writer, in the simplest "uniterm" systems of indexing, ". . . the indexer writes out a list of words from the text that he thinks are representative of the contents of the document."—Charles P. Bourne, *Methods of Information Handling* (New York, 1963), p. 15. That description is worth pondering.

[5] Archibald Leycester Clarke, *Manual of Practical Indexing,* 2nd ed. rev. (London, 1933), pp. 191, 194: "Careful indexing of statement of opinion is most certainly requisite; statement of fact is inexorable in its demands on the indexer's rigid attention to the merest detail." In indexing an historical work, "it is closeness of detail . . . that is so important. Every event in the life of an individual must be recorded under his name. The event also must appear as a separate subject-heading and the name of the person whom it affected should be entered under

ployed as well as items of all sorts named, mentioned, and referred to, provision of such a Cast for each of the writings in some field would, if anything could, make possible the compilation of a true "concept bibliography";[6] it would appear possible to list all employments of the concept of love, or all mentions of Dante, occurring in a certain set of writings. Whether the ability to identify a hundred thousand mentions of Dante or a hundred million employments of the concept of love is a desirable ability, is a question that will occupy us in the final part of this essay. It is in any case clear that no satisfactory "concept bibliography" would result from the mere fusion of all the separate Casts of Characters; the same words occurring in two lists need not have the same reference, different words need not have different references, and only the very simple will suppose that we can regularly tell when different writers are employing the very same concept. The difficulties of subject catalogs are intractable enough, but those of a "concept bibliography" are staggering.

To list all occurrences of a concept, or all mentions of an item of any sort, is, however, only in a circuitous way to make available the "individual thoughts" that may be of greatest value. The most direct way of doing that is to recognize only what is important, and ignore the rest. Commonly, when indexes are prepared for books or journals, the attempt is made, not to list everything that is mentioned at all, or every concept employed, but only items that play some at least minimally significant role in the writing, everything that meets some minimum standard of "importance."[7] We try

---

it." Cyril Cleverdon, in *Classification Research: Proceedings of the Second International Study Conference . . . 1964*, ed. Pauline Atherton, FID Pubn. no. 370 (Copenhagen, 1965), p. 448: "The highest level of exhaustivity implies the recognition of every possible concept, with the inclusion of each such concept in the index."

[6] Schneider, op. cit., p. 51: "Gedankenbibliographie," by the strictest application of which one could collect everything "was je über ein Gebiet geschrieben worden sei." "Concept bibliography" is not a very satisfactory translation, but "thought bibliography" strikes me as still worse.

[7] Clarke (op. cit., p. 22) writes the notion of importance into his definition of indexing: "The art of indexing may therefore be defined as the operation of calling attention to any item of importance in printed or non-printed matter by means of an entry which demonstrates the position of information required on any given subject." Just as librarians' manuals of cataloging say almost nothing about how one knows what the subject of a writing is, so indexers' manuals say almost nothing about how one knows what is important enough to mention. The very sensible Robert Collison's *Indexing Books, A Manual of Basic Principles* (New York, 1962), really has nothing to say about the most basic principle of all, that of listing only what is important, except to say that "Indexing is no mechanical job, and every good index is custom-made to suit a particular purpose. . . . Thus, if the work is a history of a particular locality, he [the indexer] may feel inclined to include every reference to local people, places, and events, and to restrict his entries for other subjects to the more important items

to list the named characters of the Cast, ignoring the spear-carriers and participants in crowd scenes. And in general, any indexing activity requires decision about what is worth mentioning, what is sufficiently significant in the writing to deserve recognition in the resulting index or bibliographical instrument, unless, what is surely never a real goal, one aims at absolute completeness.[8] The bases on which such decisions are made, the criteria of importance, might be divided into two groups, internal and external, or perhaps better, intrinsic and extrinsic.

When we apply intrinsic criteria of importance, or internal criteria, we view a writing much as we would an aesthetic object, and estimate the importance of an item, or of the discussion of an item, in terms of the differ-

---

only . . ." (p. 26). Where Clarke had spoken of what must be done, Collison speaks only of being "inclined." In J. W. Perry and Allen Kent's massive *Tools for Machine Literature Searching* (New York, 1958), p. 162, we read: "The first step in indexing a report is to decide what are the important characteristics of its subject matter. Such decision requires expert knowledge of the subject matter." Whether expert knowledge is indeed required is a moot point; see, for example, Costello, op cit., pp. 45 ff. Expert knowledge could not be sufficient, even if it be necessary; we cannot claim that the expert can naturally see what is important in any given paper within the field of his expertise simply because he *is* an expert. Perry and Kent do not discuss what determines importance; neither do the other writings on indexing that I have examined.

[8] Maron and Kuhns, "On Relevance, Probabilistic Indexing and Information Retrieval," *Journal of the Association for Computing Machinery*, 7 (1960), p. 221, suggest a subtly different description of what one does in indexing. They claim that "when an individual indexes a document (i.e., when he decides which terms to use to tag a document)" he intuitively estimates "the probability that if a user wants information of the kind contained in document D_i he will formulate a request by using [index term] I_j." Ordinarily he "decides" it to be simply either likely or not likely that a given term would be used, but he might be allowed to estimate *how* likely it was that a given term would be used, and reflect that estimate in the index itself, by affixing a "weight" to the tag or index term. Let us see how this claim is to be interpreted, and whether it is correct. An indexer wonders whether to assign a given writing to a position labelled "Anxiety," and to decide, he must estimate the likelihood that, if a person wants information of the sort contained in the writing, he will have requested "writings on anxiety." At first we might take this to mean that the indexer must predict the precise *wording* of the user's request; but in that case the indexer would not be worrying about whether to index or not, but what the terminology of the index should be. Nor is this the intended interpretation. Rather, the indexer's estimate is of the likelihood that, *if* the user is satisfied on receiving this writing, he will have been asking for writings on anxiety (not necessarily in those words); that is, that, on the supposition that the user is satisfied with this writing, what satisfies him is its containing material bearing on the topic of anxiety. Now whether or not indexes make "intuitive" estimates of this sort, a question on which I have no information, it seems evident that if one tried to defend such an estimate, one could do so only by showing that the writing was in fact devoted (wholly or in considerable part) to a discussion of anxiety, or that its primary utility was in its contribution to the study of anxiety. But these are quite conventional bases for indexing. It does not appear to me that Maron and Kuhns have suggested a real alternative to the customary way of describing the process of indexing: if anything, they have added an unnecessary step between estimation of the importance of a discussion and decision to represent it in an index.

ence its exclusion would have made to the writing. The importance of an item is approximately the measure of its indispensability, and to estimate that is to imagine how different the writing would have been without that item where it is. Would the picture have been perceptibly different without it, would omission of it have materially altered the story? If we try to answer such questions on the basis of internal criteria, we are supposing ourselves neutral spectators, with no special interests or particular curiosities to be satisfied. We are not looking for anything in particular, not expecting anything definite. Within limits, what seems important, that is, more or less indispensable, depends on the skill of the writer and the proportions of the story. We might at first think that the only, or at least the primary, internal criterion of importance was the mere length of a discussion of an item, and rejoice in discovering a criterion of importance whose application required no judgment and so offered no occasion for misjudgment. But in fact the length of a discussion of one thing is not much, if at all, easier to determine than the subject of a discussion. To determine the length of a discussion of a thing we must be able at each point in a writing to say "He is not (or not yet) talking about X," or "He is still talking (or has now begun to talk) about X"; but it is no easy thing to say, in general, when exactly a person begins to talk of a thing, or stops talking of it, and the boundaries of a patch of talk about some one thing are certain to be vague.[9]

In any case, length is not the only possible internal criterion of importance, nor need it be the most important; if it were the only criterion, the notion of a "brief but important discussion" would be self-contradictory, and if it were always the most important one, we could never in indexing ignore the omnipresent background items, which nevertheless we sometimes do. As the counting of references is only one way of identifying the subject of a writing, so measuring the length of discussions is only one (and a nonmechanical) way of deciding importance, even when a writing is looked at entirely from the "inside."

---

[9] In the very simplest cases, we can say: "Here is the first mention of X; each of the next n sentences also mentions X, and after that there are no more mentions of X." But such ludicrously simple cases are hard to find in actual writings; the "natural" way to write or talk involves constant illustration, comparison, digression, qualification and so on, with the result that a sustained discussion of one thing is by no means a simple series of repeated references to that thing. Much of the discussion in Chapter V above applies here, for instance that of indirect references.

Indexing is not, of course, always done from the "inside," on the basis of internal or intrinsic criteria of importance. When we apply extrinsic or external criteria, we judge the importance of an item, not in terms of how much its exclusion would have meant to the writing, but in terms of how much its exclusion would have meant to us, or to those we represent. We look at it with interests, goals, a background of theory and fact, and importance now means importance *to* one with such equipment. An indexer who knows the active interests of some group of people will count as important enough to mention whatever he thinks would be seized on by one with those interests. So the historian of a place will be alive to mentions of that place, its inhabitants, its visitors; the historian of technology will be alive to discussions of apparatus of all sorts, of artificers, of instructions for making apparatus, which would interest no one else. The length of a discussion is, from the outside, perfectly irrelevant, has no bearing on one's decision; a short mention of some item of interest to the indexer's intended clientele will be recognized, a long discussion of what falls outside their range of interests will be quite ignored. Of course there is no reason why indexing must be done entirely on the basis of internal criteria, or of external, and both will presumably be used at once.

Internal criteria are those whose application requires looking at nothing but the writing being judged; external criteria are those whose application requires looking beyond the writing itself. Now one may look beyond in many different directions: to other writings, to the interests of particular men and groups of men, to standards and goals shared by many men or few. There is an important practical, if not theoretical, distinction to be made among relatively impersonal and relatively personal external considerations, a distinction which would be reflected in our saying of some writings that they were important *to* this man or that man, and of other writings that they were, simply, important. If I have goals and interests that happen to be shared by few others or by no others, then a piece of writing may be of utmost importance to me, while of no importance to anyone else, hence not important simpliciter. We might, on the other hand, call a piece of writing important because of its novelty (its "serious" novelty, for anyone can be novel if he is willing to be frivolous, but we are not inclined to count as important what we take to be frivolous); novelty is not an "intrinsic" character, we cannot spot novelty unless we know what has

Indexing, Coupling, Hunting

already been written, but then it is not one whose detection requires looking at the situations of any men, and so is a relatively "impersonal" feature. And if we call a piece of writing important because we think it says profound and true things, we again look beyond the writing itself, but do not look at any particular individual's interests and goals. It is possible and finally, I think, necessary to argue that at bottom *all* the external criteria of importance reflect the interests, standards, goals of particular individuals, but there is still the practical difference between what is important because of the possession of characteristics that all men, or all scholars or all of some other considerable group value, and what is important because of the possession of characteristics that matter to only one man, or a few.

It is to be presumed that the criteria of importance one uses in indexing will make a difference to one's work, that the result of the application of internal criteria exclusively will differ from the result of the application of impersonal external criteria, and from the result of the application of criteria that are more or less idiosyncratic or personal. In the first of these cases the indexer takes on, as it were, the role of a literary critic, treating the writing as a story and estimating what is largely and what is minimally contributory to the story. Or he is like an editor, trying to shorten a manuscript; the things which cannot be cut out are the things that require representation by the indexer. In the second case, the indexer is the impersonal representative of humanity at large, or of scholars in general, or of those who pursue some distinct line of work, while in the third he is the personal representative of some particular men. Now evidently something like the problem of the "sense of position" of the last chapter appears here as well, for unless we know what the indexer thinks it is that makes a writing, or a discussion in a writing, important, we do not know what it means to find an item marked as important. Finding an item at a place, marked "Very Important," when we are ignorant of the criteria on the basis of which importance is determined, can arouse in us only vague expectations of something in some way remarkable, but we could have no definite expectations of what the remarkability consisted in. Thus we could have only the "thinnest" sort of understanding of the index, and only the vaguest sense of position.

This problem would be overcome, were it possible to draw up exhaustive lists of the features and considerations on which importance depended. But what makes indexing an "art" is in part simply the fact that this cannot be done, even in the "hardest," most rigorous sciences. We can give long lists of examples of things to look for, but at the end of our list we must say "and so forth," trusting to the wit of the indexer to extend the list, or to see how it could be extended.[10] Of course we cannot expect that, even when the criteria to be used are stated, the indexer will always be able properly to apply them; nor can we expect that different indexers will apply them in the very same ways. These are commonplaces.[11] It is not quite so much a commonplace that we cannot even give exhaustive statements of the criteria to be employed, that we cannot give complete instructions to an indexer detailing all the things he is to take into account in his work. But if we cannot tell *him*, he cannot tell *us*; if we can give no general and complete instructions, he can give no general and complete interpretation of his work either. Only if he affixed, to each listing of an important item, a statement of what made that item important, could we know what to expect in particular cases, and in that case our understanding would not be of the sense of the position as such, but only of the reasons for inclusion of a particular item.

Suppose, now, that a bibliographical instrument is made in which, for some field of writings, it is attempted to exhibit the "individual thoughts that outweigh whole books, periodical articles, or chapters." Surely such an instrument cannot satisfactorily be made on the basis of internal criteria alone; what makes a tiny fragment of discussion of outstanding importance is not simply its looming large in its particular context, considered in isolation from all other writings and from all goals and interests and standards.

---

[10] Such a list is given, for instance, in *Chemical Abstracts,* 39 (1945), 5868. This is a partial list of "factors" that must be considered in "deciding on subject entries to be made for an abstract."

[11] It is universally recognized that equally intelligent and scrupulous indexers will not produce identical results when working on the same materials; why is this so, if not because of the impossibility of exhaustive listing of relevant factors and precise instructions for recognizing their presence and "degree"? Related difficulties obviously exist in the cases of abstracting and of the calendaring of manuscripts. See, for instance, the remarks of J. C. Fitzpatrick in *Notes on the Care, Cataloguing, Calendaring and Arranging of Manuscripts,* 2nd ed. (Washington, D.C.: Library of Congress, 1921), p. 30: calendaring, that is, providing "briefs of the contents" of manuscripts, "has the disadvantage too of being tinctured with the personality of the calendarer; for, while a calendar of the same manuscript by two experts would record the same major subjects of the document, these would be presented somewhat differently and, often perhaps, in such form as to give entirely different emphasis to the same fact; the variations in the minor subjects meanwhile, showing still greater differences." What is said of calendaring applies, by obvious analogy, to the making of abstracts. Fitzpatrick gives, incidentally, an elegant and instructive pair of examples of briefs of the same short letter, on pp. 33–34.

Then external criteria must be employed. But while the application of impersonal external criteria may reveal much of what would otherwise be unnoticed, impersonal criteria cannot be counted on to reveal what is of supreme importance for any given individual. There is nothing surprising in this: unless the work of indexing is done not only *for* me but on the basis of an intimate knowledge of my interests and requirements, the work cannot be guaranteed to identify what is important to me. No matter how intelligible the work, how clear the sense of its positions, and how well made, how reliable or trustworthy in the application of its chosen criteria, unless those criteria reflect my interests and requirements, the result can not be guaranteed to pick out what is of greatest importance to me. It may of course manage by accident to do so, but it could not be counted on to do so. And what is true for me is true for everyone else; a splendidly made instrument, using impersonal external criteria of importance, might suit no one at all, for while it identified what everyone would admit was important, it identified nothing that was important to any particular individual. We hope this will not often happen; but we must admit that it might.

Unless, then, indexing is done specifically for me, and on the basis of intimate knowledge of my interests and requirements, it is likely that I shall always have to engage in exploration, in searching, for the things that are most important to me. Indeed, in any but the hypothetically completely exhaustive "concept bibliography," we may find it necessary to explore, or search, for things which have not been collected or arranged or identified in a fashion that suits our purposes. Let us now see what can be said in general about such exploration.

If I understand the organization of a bibliographical instrument, in that I know what positions are available and what are the rules of assignment to position, then I know what I can do *immediately* with the instrument, subject, of course, to questions of reliability. The items listed have been sorted out for me in various ways, which may or may not be ways in which I would like them sorted out; and so I am in a position to identify immediately the works listed that are, say, written in Finnish, or published before 1800, or "on the topic" of the introduction of the stirrup into Western Europe. It requires no work on my part to identify these things, for they have been already identified for me. But in addition to the things I can do immediately, there are things I can do *mediately:* depending on what sort of description is given of the items listed, I can identify, among the items at some position, all those which satisfy various further conditions beyond the conditions for assignment to that position. Among the many ways in which I may find the content of items revealed by description, these are perhaps worth recalling. We may find an "informative abstract" or précis, compressing what is said in many words into few. We may find an outline of the writing, showing the structure of the composition or the sequence of primary topics or characters. We may find a sample of the writing, a continuous segment or several brief segments. We may find a reproduction of the table of contents or a list of chapter headings. We may find a summary of conclusions, or a characterization of the "point of view," of sources from which the writing derives, of influences it exhibits, of the school or faction it represents, of its animus or bias. Description is of course not limited to description of content; indeed, most bibliographical instruments give shockingly little description of content, position being the only indication, other than the title of the writing,[12] of what is in the writing. Whatever the sort of description given, if it is given systematically, it allows us to make identifications of members of various classes of writings, beyond those classes already picked out by the organizational device.

If I am unable to identify the members of some set of writings either immediately or mediately, either on the basis of location or on the basis of descriptions given, still I may be able to make reasonable guesses about the membership of that set, on the basis of what I know about the organizational scheme, about the world in general, about the history of scholarship, about the habits of bibliographers and catalogers. I may be able to say that items of the sort I am looking for are more likely to be at position N_1 and position N_2 than anywhere else, or that things described in this way are more likely to be of the sort I want than things described in any other way. My guesses may be good or bad (which is not the same as being correct or incorrect), informed or uninformed; but guesses are the only way of discovering items fitting a certain description which are not explicitly or implicitly assigned that description already. If the word "guess" suggests too strongly a total want of reason for one opinion rather than another, we may substitute another, and speak of forming opinions about the likelihood of locating items at a position, rather than of guessing the location of items.

---

[12] But for some purposes the title may suffice. See A. Resnick, "Relative Effectiveness of Document Titles and Abstracts for Determining Relevance of Documents," *Science*, 134 (6 Oct. 1961), 1004–1006.

Indexing, Coupling, Hunting 103

But it is no matter; I may have little basis for expecting to find the things I seek in one place rather than another, or I may have the best reasons in the world, and my predictions about where I shall find what I seek may range from unsupported wild surmises to the soundest and most massively supported inductive inferences.

A person trying to predict the most likely location in which to find items of a certain sort can be said to be *hunting*;[13] and one trying to select items of that sort on the basis of the descriptions given, when the descriptions are inadequate for definite identification of the items, can be said to be *picking*. The aim of the makers of bibliographical instruments, in choosing one sort of organization over another, and choosing to include one set of descriptive items rather than another, is presumably to minimize the amount of hunting and picking that the users of their work will have to do, to select the sort of organization that will fit most closely the patterns of interest of the intended or expected users and to provide sufficient information to allow mediate selection in most if not all cases. But this can never be more than a lucky result, for there is no way of predicting what people will want to do next. We cannot eliminate the need for hunting and picking, for we cannot anticipate all the ways in which people will ask for the items we list in bibliographical instruments.

Let us have an illustration for this overly abstract account of hunting and picking. Suppose I want to find, in a large bibliography or catalog arranged according to the Dewey Decimal Classification,[14] whatever writings there are that discuss the history of the use of the stirrup. My want is no more exact than that; I do not want only those books whose unique subject is the history of the stirrup, nor only those writings in which there are at least five mentions of stirrups, but simply, whatever writings there are that discuss the history of the use of the stirrup. It happens that I shall find no position whose description includes specific mention of stirrups; but even if I did find such a position, I would only be at the beginning of my search,

---

[13] What I am calling "hunting" is not to be identified either with that "translation into the language of the indexing system" which is so continuously, and so misleadingly, talked of in writings on information retrieval, nor with what is described as the formulation of "search strategies," though it is clearly akin to what is commonly described under the latter heading. "Translation" is a badly misleading term for what is commonly an attempt at formulating a suitable substitute for the request one would like to make but cannot make. "Search strategies" may include both instances of hunting and of complex but still, in my terms, *immediate* uses of an instrument.

[14] Seventeenth edition. I use this merely as an example, for the sake of definiteness.

if assignment were to only a single position and made on the basis of identification of the unique subject of the items to be located.

How do I decide where, or where else, to look for writings containing discussions of the history of the use of the stirrup? I find a position whose description runs: "Harnesses and accessories of livestock and domestic animals" and another with the description: "Harnesses and accessories of horses." But I also find positions described so: "Cavalry equipment and supplies," "History of cavalry," "Horsemanship," "History of technology." There are hundreds of other available positions, from among which I choose these as more likely than others to be occupied by writings containing the sort of discussion I want. In making this choice, I employ whatever knowledge I have, not only of the system of classification but of the world, of things, and of scholarship. I know that the stirrup is something to which the phrase "harnesses and accessories" applies, that the horse is a domestic animal, that cavalry are or used to be military forces mounted on horseback, that horsemanship is the art of riding, that the history of technology includes the study of things like stirrups. Even to begin my search, I must know elementary facts like these. But the more I know, about stirrups and horses and warfare and scholarship, the better I can choose the positions in which to look for the discussions I seek. If I know that the stirrup was introduced into France in the eighth century, I shall add to my list of positions to be examined some of those into whose description "France" enters, particularly positions whose descriptions include reference to technology and warfare. Similarly for other countries and times. I also might know enough of the history of scholarship to avoid certain positions, or to rank them low with respect to the likelihood of their containing writings with discussions of the sort I want. I might avoid modern regimental cavalry histories on the ground that what I knew of the habits of regimental historians made it appear most unlikely that any would digress to discuss the history of the stirrup, though no sort of digression is in principle impossible.

Having selected a number of positions as being more likely than others to contain writings with discussions of the sort I want, I then examine the descriptions of the items listed at each of those positions. From the descriptions given, I may be able to identify some items as certainly containing such discussions, for abstracts or lists of chapter headings may provide conclusive evidence. Even when conclusive evidence is lacking, I may be able

Indexing, Coupling, Hunting 105

to make reasonable guesses about which items are most likely to contain such discussions: if a title read "Mounted Shock Combat and the Temper of Feudal Life," or if a chapter heading read "Stirrup, Mounted Shock Combat, Feudalism, and Chivalry," I would think the items worth examination. And in many less obvious ways the descriptions may provide clues, from which good guesses about the identity of works with the right sort of discussion can be made. Again, the more I know, about the world and about the habits of scholars, the better able I am to make good guesses; a description that suggests nothing to the ignorant may be a powerful clue to the wise. Of course even the wisest hunter and picker cannot be certain of finding all there is to find; we may, by hunting and picking, in fact find all there is to find, but we cannot know that we have done so.[15]

We have so far spoken of the organizational component of the Specifications of a bibliographical instrument as consisting simply of a repertory of places; while this is true in many cases, large and complex organizational components are likely to include an auxiliary apparatus, in the form of indexes to places, of thesauri of descriptive terms, of "cross references" from one place to another. The auxiliary apparatus has, it appears, two principal purposes. The first is that of partially compensating for the fact that a very complex organizational scheme may be so complex that none of the users of instruments in which it is applied knows, or can be expected to know, what positions are available. The auxiliary apparatus functions as a guide to the contents of the repertory of positions, supplementing the basic or "canonical" list which is, perhaps, too long to be scanned in its entirety each time a person wants to use it.[16]

---

[15] My example was chosen somewhat maliciously. Lynn White, Jr., *Medieval Technology and Social Change* (Oxford, 1962), contains one chapter (of its total of three) on "Stirrup, Mounted Shock Combat, Feudalism, and Chivalry," of which a large part discusses the history of the use of the stirrup. The Library of Congress assigned the subject headings "Civilization, Medieval" and "Technology and Civilization" to the book and suggested the Dewey number 901.92, Medieval Civilization.

[16] "In binding related headings together the basic rule is that a 'see also' reference be made from a given subject: (1) to more specific subjects or topics comprehended within it, or to an application of the subject; and (2) to coordinate subjects which suggest themselves as likely to be of interest to the user seeking material under the given heading, because they represent other aspects of the subject, or are closely related to it. The suggestive element of the heading is important in that the reader may not be fully aware of the scope of the heading he is looking under."—David Judson Haykin, *Subject Headings, A Practical Guide* (Washington, D.C., 1951), pp. 14–15. But beyond the "suggestive element," what reason is there for such connective tissue in the catalog? Haykin says no more, and even Cutter, who tries to give sufficient reasons for doing things one way rather than another, is disappointing on this question: "From *Cathedrals*, for example, one would naturally refer to *Christian art* and to *Ecclesiastical*

The second purpose is that of facilitating hunting, providing suggestions, as it were, to one who, not having found what he wanted, or all of what he wanted, at one position, is uncertain about where to go next. The customary apparatus consists of a system of what we can call *couplings* of positions,[17] as well as of alternative descriptions of single positions ("see" references). Links or connections between positions are established, which may be of three sorts. The first sort include what might be called "analytic" couplings, connections between positions which reflect logical or semantical relationships between rules of assignment to the positions coupled. If one position is described in terms of one sort of thing or "subject," and another in terms of another, and we can see simply by reflection on the meanings of the terms describing those things that one is a species or kind or part or aspect of the other, then the positions can be analytically coupled. We know without need of investigation that steamships are ships, the cavalry a branch of the armed forces, horses animals, and Percherons horses. But it is not only relations of species to genus that we discover by reflection on meanings of terms, for the necessary relationship between horsemanship and horses is not such a relationship, yet as easily discovered. And it is not only relations among "subjects," that is, among things that writings are about, that can be reflected by couplings of positions; any characteristics of things on the

---

architecture, because works on those subjects will contain more or less on cathedrals. But so will histories of architecture and histories of English, French, German, Italian, or Spanish architecture; so will travels in England, France, Germany, Italy, Spain. And anyone who desired to take an absolutely complete survey of the subject, or who was willing to spend unlimited time in getting information on some detail, would have to consult such books. Yet the cataloguer may very excusably not think of referring to those subjects, or if he thinks of it may deem the connection too remote to justify reference, and that he should be overloading the catalog with what would be generally useless."—Charles A. Cutter, *Rules for a Dictionary Catalog* (Washington, 1904), p. 80. Then why refer to Christian art and Ecclesiastical architecture? Of course it is "out of the question to make all possible references of the ascending kind," as Cutter says, and nowadays it is supposed never to be done at all, even though "the very best description of a single plant or of a family of plants may perhaps be contained in a botanical encyclopaedia," and analogously for all other topics. I think it safe to say there is *no* rationale for present library practice in the making of references from one heading to another.

[17] Not, of course, to be confused with the "bibliographic coupling" discussed by M. M. Kessler in, for instance, "Bibliographic Coupling between Scientific Papers," *American Documentation,* 14 (1963), 10–25. What he discusses is a relationship between particular writings; what I am concerned with is relationships among the abstract positions of an organizational scheme, or rather, with explicit indications of some of the relationships that exist whether recognized or not. It should be noted that within a classified system of positions, couplings are made by typographical or notational devices exhibiting relationships of "subordination." The purpose of a classified arrangement of positions is clearly not merely to help the hunter or show the ignorant what positions are available, though hunting might be sometimes easier in a classified scheme.

basis of which they are assigned to positions in an organizational scheme may have parallel analytic relationships. Horses are a species of animal, and books with red covers are a species of books whose covers are of primary colors, and an analytic coupling could as readily be made between positions described in terms of the latter odd distinguishing feature as between positions described in terms of the subjects of horses and animals.

The second sort of coupling includes what we might call factual couplings, or (reflecting the conventional philosophic distinction) "synthetic" couplings. That Pierpont Morgan was a banker, that diamonds are used in industry to cut things, that redwood trees are used to provide lumber from which houses and furniture are made, all of these are matters of fact which might be reflected in couplings among positions. They are facts which relate "subjects," and any matter of fact connection between "subjects" might in theory be reflected by a factual or "synthetic" coupling. The coupling might exhibit the sort of factual connection, might indicate that one position was described in terms of what was in fact an instance or application or effect or by-product of what the other position was described in terms of; or the coupling might be uninformative, indicative merely of some sort of factual connection (as in some ordinary "see also" references).

The third sort of coupling might be called the "overlap" sort of coupling. To establish the first two sorts, one needs read no books at all, or no particular books; such couplings could be established simply on the basis of reflection on the meanings of the terms used in the rules of application, or on the basis of "common knowledge." But one might establish a coupling of positions on the basis of examination of the writings assigned those positions, and of a discovery of a degree of overlapping of content. Writings assigned position N_1 might characteristically contain the same sort of talk as those assigned position N_2, perhaps because of an "association" of topics that has little or no basis in factual or analytic connections of the topics discussed. Books assigned a position described in terms of, say, the history of Sanskrit literature might characteristically overlap in content with those assigned a position described in terms of the history of Indian medicine, where works "on" the history of Greek literature might characteristically *not* overlap in content with those "on" the history of Greek medicine, and this for, as we would say, "accidental" reasons of the history of scholarship. Of course we can imagine other sorts of connection among the writings assigned different positions that might be the basis for coupling; but the actual overlap of content is the most obvious sort of connection.[18]

The difference between the first and second sort of coupling is clear enough in principle but vague in practice.[19] Is it a matter of the meaning of terms, or of widely known fact, that would allow coupling positions described in terms of bread and food? It may be that we cannot invariably say whether the descriptions of two positions have analytic or only factual

---

[18] See note 17 above. The notion of the overlap coupler is akin to but not identical with the statistical relationships discussed by Maron and Kuhns (op. cit., pp. 252ff.), as their "automatic groping in index space" is akin to hunting. They propose connecting terms (our positions) on the basis of the frequencies with which pairs of terms have been assigned the same items. One can imagine other frequency measures: instead of counting the number of items that have been assigned to both of a given pair of positions, to derive a measure of "closeness of connection" between the positions, we can imagine comparing the vocabularies, in a purely formal way, of all or a random sample of writings assigned to two different positions (different writings, not the same) and noting the degree of overlap. Kessler's bibliographic coupling is another applicable way of connecting positions: if writings listed at position A tend to be bibliographically coupled with (that is, briefly, share common references to other writings) those at B, and more strongly coupled with those at B than with those at C, then the "strength of coupling" between A and B is greater than that between A and C, and if above some minimum figure, could be explicitly exhibited. But these two are mechanically determinable substitutes for our overlap couplers; the overlap couplers say that writings at different positions contain the same sort of discussions, while these say that they contain the same (or some of the same) words, or refer to (some of) the same items, hence are more or less likely to overlap in content. Maron and Kuhns' procedure, on the other hand, seems a curious argument from analogy: since so many writings have been assigned positions A and B in the past, those assigned A but not B may indeed also contain material like that in those assigned both A and B. But if they do, why were they not assigned both A and B?

[19] This will be violently disputed by many; for years there has raged a controversy among philosophers and logicians about the "analytic-synthetic" distinction, a controversy which is not over nor likely soon to be so. W. V. O. Quine's "Two Dogmas of Empiricism" in his *From a Logical Point of View* (Cambridge, Mass., 1953), pp. 20–46, can conveniently be taken as the starting point of recent discussion. Many of the more important papers are mentioned by Quine in his *Word and Object* (New York, 1960), see especially p. 67, fn. 7. The dispute is, roughly, over whether the difference between analytic and synthetic is one of kind or of degree.

In that curious work of J. C. R. Licklider, *Libraries of the Future* (Cambridge, Mass, 1965), pp. 61–62, it is claimed that with the help of an "effective, formal, analytical semantics," it would be possible to construct "networks" in the "fund of knowledge" in which every element of that fund would be connected to every other element to which it was "significantly related," and showing the type of relationship and its degree. If "semantics" is meant as the study of meaning, this amounts to the Leibnizian claim that all truths are necessary truths, and that to know the meaning of any term is to know all the truths into the statement of which that term enters. It is generally conceded nowadays that such a claim is preposterous. One simply cannot discover truths about electricity by reflecting on the meaning of the word "electricity," and no amount of semantic analysis of that and other terms would suffice to show the connections between electricity and, say, therapy. This is true, whatever the outcome of the argument over the analytic-synthetic distinction.

For a different sort of discussion of the relationships that might be reflected in couplings, see B. C. Vickery, *On Retrieval System Theory* (London, 1961), chap. 4, and the writings there referred to.

Indexing, Coupling, Hunting

connections, whether there is a necessary or only a factual connection between the things described at the two positions. The difference is, however, of some theoretical importance, for analytic couplers are dispensable in a way in which factual ones are not.[20]

A person who understood the rules of assignment of an organizational device would, in theory, have no need of analytic couplers, for the connections among positions thereby established would already be known to him, or could become known simply by reflection. To one who does not know the rules of assignment, analytic couplers may help establish the senses of positions; he partially discovers what it means about an item that it is assigned this position by noting what other positions are connected with it by the coupling device. But for him who understands the scheme and its rules, such analytic couplers reflect only what he already knows or can discover without their help, by simple reflection.

The factual or "synthetic" couplers are not in that way dispensable, for a person might in principle understand the rules of assignment perfectly yet lack the factual knowledge about the world which such couplers reflect. And the less the knowledge they represent is a matter of "common knowledge," the less dispensable they are, the more they add to the power of the whole organizational scheme. But there are countless possible factual couplers, for there are countless factual connections among items described in the rules of assignment. Which of the myriad relationships that any one thing has with other things shall be reflected by couplers? Horsemanship is related to blacksmithing and to sports in obvious ways, as to a thousand or a million other things; no organizational auxiliary device can reflect all the relationships among the "subjects" it recognizes, and so a selection must be made: but how? The easy answer is to say: let it reflect the closest relationships among subjects, and ignore the remote. But this answer is almost empty of meaning, until it is specified which of the endlessly many relationships among things we are to consider and how we are to arrive at a conclusion about overall closeness of relationship on the basis of tens or hundreds or thousands of statements of particular relationships.

Some, but by no means all, relationships of things allow more or less precise statement of "distance"; spatial and temporal relationships are ex-

---

[20] What is dispensable in theory may be essential in practice. The larger and more complex an organizational scheme, the harder it is for anyone to master and the more useful couplers, even analytic couplers, become. But they are still theoretically uninteresting.

amples, as are kinship relationships of persons. The all important relationship of similarity is one which allows only vague "qualitative" measures; we cannot in general compare two things and say precisely how similar they are, as we might be able to say how far apart they are in space or time. Many relationships do not admit of degree at all; the relationship of part to whole, or ingredient to mixture, seem not to do so. But even if we had compiled what we thought to be an exhaustive catalog of the relationships in which a thing stood to each of several others, with statements of the closeness of each particular relationship whenever possible, there would be no single, natural way in which to derive a figure representing "overall closeness of relationship," no single, natural way in which even to rank the items as more or less closely related.

In our vague, intuitive estimates of this sort we rely heavily on our sense of the greater or lesser importance of particular relationships, and what is important in one connection will not be so in another. (This is one reason for the impossibility of making a single, perfectly satisfactory classification scheme.) The general instruction to "connect only the most closely related subjects" seems appealing, perhaps, because we obscurely think of "being related" as itself a simple, directly measurable relationship; the instruction loses its attractiveness when we begin to reflect that there are indefinitely many particular relationships to be considered, and indefinitely many ways of assigning importance to particular relationships and "adding" them up to arrive at estimates of "overall closeness of relationship." Estimates of this sort are likely to be as numerous as the people making them.

But let us suppose that we could devise a method that would allow us to identify, for each subject or topic represented in a repertory of positions, the five or ten or hundred most closely related positions, in order of their closeness of relationship. Suppose the related positions coupled in such a way that we could automatically pick out the position most closely related to any given position, then proceed to the next most closely related, and so on. What good would this do us? It must be that there is what we might call a "General Rule of Hunting" which goes something like this: Discussions of a thing X are more likely to be found in the context of discussions of a thing Y, the more closely related Y is to X. Any two things whatever might be discussed together, but, other things being equal, it is more reasonable to expect things to be discussed together, the more closely related they are. Only a madman would think that discussions of the history of the stirrup were more likely to be found among discussions of dentistry or dandelions than among discussions of cavalry or equestrianism. The rule has great intuitive plausibility, so long as we ask no embarrassing questions about how degrees of closeness of relationship are to be established. But, in addition to those questions, there are a couple of fairly obvious truths that must be recalled.

In the first place, that discussions of a certain sort are more likely to be found in one place than another does not mean that they are likely to be found in either place, that is, "appreciably" likely. And that discussions are unlikely to appear at a given place does not at all mean that they will not appear there, for the unlikely is not the impossible. Nor is the likely the necessary, so what is likely may nevertheless not occur. If our desire is not to collect all the discussions of a topic that there are in a body of writings, but only a few, or a representative collection, factual couplers may be of little help, for we may find little or no more by examining the writings at the most closely related place. If our desire is to collect all the discussions there are, to exhaust a body of writings of its discussions of some topic, then we shall have to go beyond the most closely related positions, for there is no rule or principle that says that all the discussions of a topic are to be found among the writings on the five or ten or hundred most closely related topics. But most important of all, what is likely when judged on the basis of this general rule of hunting may be exceedingly unlikely in the light of other knowledge or evidence at one's disposal. This rule would be a proper rule for one to follow who knew nothing of the subject he was pursuing; but the more one knows about the subject one is pursuing, and about the history of the study of that subject, the more knowledge one has on which to base estimates of likelihood of what one seeks being here or there. For couplings based on estimates of closeness of relationships are, insofar as they are aids to hunting, only substitutes for couplings based on discoveries of actual overlap of content among writings at different places; they serve as estimates of the likelihood that overlap of content will be found.[21] One's knowledge of the history of scholarship may allow one to make better estimates of the likelihood of overlap of content. An auxiliary apparatus would be preferable that discovered and noted actual overlaps, that consisted of "overlap" couplers rather than of analytic or factual ones.[22] (This is one of the most amiable features of some bibliographies, which will say,

---

[21] Unless, that is, one is looking for writings with a certain *utility* rather than a certain content. Compare the remarks on the second rule of hunting at the end of this chapter.

[22] But more "exhaustive" indexing would no doubt be preferable to any elaboration of the auxiliary apparatus.

at various places, "Further discussions of this topic will be found among such and such types of works," or some variation of this.)

But, again, no bibliographer can provide such apparatus as will allow identification of works under all possible descriptions, and thus hunting will always be necessary. Nor is there a single rule of hunting that might lead to optimal results in every case, though it would be easy enough to formulate rules of hunting which, used as the sole rule, would have much worse results than that given above. In hunting for discussions, or writings of one or another type, one uses whatever knowledge one has that is relevant, i.e., that favors one hypothesis over another. The more knowledge one has, the better one is likely to do, and the experienced scholar is almost certain to be able to achieve better results in a shorter time at hunting than is the novice or the poorly informed. The scholar who knows that two topics now thought to be closely related were not previously thought closely related will adjust his hunting accordingly, and he who knows that what is now thought not at all closely related to his topic was previously thought closely related will do so as well. The good hunter is one with a great deal of accumulated knowledge and experience of the history and habits of scholars, of the fashions and tendencies of thought and investigation, the preferences and predilections of scholars of different ages and traditions, all of which knowledge and experience he uses, perhaps without conscious formulation, in his estimates of likelihood. The good hunter is the knowledgeable hunter, and the knowledge he uses is knowledge both about the things people write about and about the history of scholarship and the habits of writers.

All of this is no doubt obvious on reflection; these are elementary facts about hunting and exploring in general.[28] But it seems worthwhile to recall obvious facts, since otherwise one might suppose that a bibliographical instrument might be supplied with such auxiliary apparatus as would inevitably direct the ignorant user to the writings he asks for, even when what he asks for has not already been identified and collected at one

---

[28] "The work of prospecting is usually left to adventurous men who are willing to undergo privation and hardship in the hope of large reward though the chances of success are small. The prospector is guided in his search by a knowledge of the geological conditions under which useful minerals occur. When the rocks are concealed by detrital material he looks for outcroppings on steep hillsides, on the crests of hills or ridges . . . Sometimes the vegetation, shrubs, trees, &c., as characteristic of certain soils, may furnish evidence as to rock or minerals below. . . . It must be remembered that the line between a workable deposit and one that cannot be profitably worked is often very narrow and that the majority of mineral deposits are not workable."—*Encyclopaedia Britannica*, 11th ed., s.v. *mining*.

Indexing, Coupling, Hunting

position or a set of positions, or sufficiently identified by the descriptions furnished for each item listed. It might have been thought that a sufficiently elaborate set of "cross-references" would have eliminated the need of hunting, or have made it invariably successful, as it might have been thought that by providing many clues to the content of writings, picking could be made invariably successful. But clues must be recognized as such; they cannot be intelligibly labeled "clue." And only the knowledgeable man can profit from clues, can know what to make of them. And, if it is true that what I have called analytic and factual couplers are only substitutes for what I have called "overlap" couplers, the former are clearly not equivalent in effect to the latter, are not perfect substitutes. As aids to the ignorant, the auxiliary apparatus of analytic and factual couplers have value; but they are only aids, not guarantors of successful hunting.

We began by asking what sort of bibliographical instrument was most suitable for making available the "individual thoughts that outweigh whole books, periodical articles, or chapters," and came to a discussion of hunting by reflection on the likely insufficiency of any attempt at direct identification of the important thoughts and discussions. What has been said about aids to hunting applies primarily to a search for writings resembling in subject matter rather than in utility; the "General Rule of Hunting" suggested above does not seem a sensible one to follow, if one is attempting to find good textual means to an end in an instrument in which assignment to position is made on the basis of content or subject matter rather than on the basis of utility. (If writings sharing certain features of subject matter fail to furnish suitable textual means, why look for more of the same?) We can indeed give another general rule: good textual means to the attainment of one end are the more likely to be found among those furnishing good textual means to the attainment of another end, the more similar the two ends or goals are. A Bibliographical Encyclopedia might be provided with an apparatus of couplers analogous to those described above, which best fit an instrument like that we have called The Catalog; in the Encyclopedia, the "overlaps" revealed would be of utility, not of content. It should need no argument that any attempt at such an auxiliary apparatus for a work like The Encyclopedia could at best be tentative and suggestive. If successful hunting for writings resembling in content cannot be guaranteed by any set of auxiliary devices, even less can successful hunting for writings furnishing textual means to given ends be guaranteed by such devices.

Chapter VII

CONSULTANTS AND AIDS

LET US TURN now from instruments, their organization and their use, to consider the bibliographical information that a man may possess. A man will be more or less well acquainted with, remember more or less vividly, be able to describe more or less accurately and fully, some number of writings; and there are indefinitely many more writings which he will in the past have been acquainted with, or which he will have read or heard about, but which he will no longer remember. Let us consider what he now remembers as being analogous to what a bibliography lists, and the total of what he both remembers and has forgotten as analogous to the domain of a bibliography. The analogy is imperfect, for remembering is only partly similar to deliberate selection from a domain; but the analogy is there, for a man is more likely to recall what seemed to him important or valuable than he is to recall what seemed to him trivial or empty or insignificant. He is, to be sure, more likely to remember the very bad as well as the very good, than to remember the neither very bad nor very good. But in any case his remembering is not entirely haphazard, but rather, to a greater or lesser degree, selective according to interest and estimate of value.

The analogy is further imperfect in that writings are not simply remembered or forgotten, as they are either listed or not listed in a bibliography; items are more or less available to recall, subject to more or less vivid stimuli. Despite the imperfections of the analogy, however, cannot we imagine evaluating a person's remembered store of bibliographical information in a way analogous to that in which we would evaluate a bibliography? We might say, this man's store of information is more valuable than that man's, in part simply because this man has encountered more writings than that man; which is comparable to calling one bibliography more valuable than another, because based on a larger domain. To the selection principles of a bibliographical instrument there correspond, more or less closely, the interests of a man; an interest serves as a selection principle, for what appeals to an interest has more chance of being examined and, if found valuable, remembered than what does not appeal to an interest. But an interest does more than work in this more or less passive way; for the stronger an interest, the more likely that it will lead a man to look for, or be on the lookout for, things that appeal to that interest wherever he is. It will act in the way of making one deliberately extend one's "domain" in a certain direction, deliberately seek out items that might appeal to it. A man's interests will also determine, in part, what he will remember about the writings he encounters, and how much he will remember, though mere strength or tenacity of memory also counts, and a man with a good memory for detail, even what is to him irrelevant detail, may retain a stock of what is to others valuable bibliographical information.

The value of a man's store of bibliographical information depends not only on how widely he has read and how much he remembers of what he has read or heard of, but on how deeply, carefully, critically, reflectively, comparatively he has read. A wide but superficial acquaintance may not be without value to others, for superficiality may be just what we want in some cases; but we naturally and rightly praise the man who is thought to have a deep as well as a wide knowledge of texts. I said earlier that the possession of bibliographical control in its higher degrees is to be compared with mastery of texts; and a man who is in fact a master of some body of texts is one who has, and can give us, some degree of bibliographical control over those texts. The field of competence of a man, the field of study or of activity of whose literature he is master, is the field over which his knowledge, if available to us, gives us control.

Let us call any person to whom we can put bibliographical questions with the reasonable hope of getting an answer that is adapted to our situation, a bibliographical *consultant*. Of course we might ask bibliographical questions of any one at all, but in most cases we would get no answer at all, or no intelligible or intelligent one, or no positive or correct one, or one not suited to our situation. Eminence as an intellectual worker need not make a man a good bibliographical consultant, for an eminent creator might read little, and remember little of what he read, but rather absorb what he found useful and forget its origins. Even breadth and depth of bibliographical knowledge, of mastery of texts, need not make one a good consultant, or not a generally good consultant, for a person might be unable to adopt the standpoint of another and see what would suit his purpose.

As there are persons of wide superficial bibliographical knowledge who will, when asked a question about writings, overwhelm the questioner with torrents of information useless because not suited to the questioner's wants, so there are great scholars who cannot remember that others are more ignorant of, and less interested in, their field than they are, and so cannot answer simple questions simply. The distinctive feature of the good bibliographical consultant is his ability to draw on his store of bibliographical knowledge to give advice that is appropriate to the advisee's abilities and desires and interests. A man of less bibliographical knowledge may be a better bibliographical consultant than one of greater knowledge; the knowledge represents the store from which he draws in trying to formulate a suitable answer to a question, but having a large store of knowledge does not guarantee the ability to formulate suitable answers. A man full of bibliographical information about a field, and willing to tell us all he knows, does indeed give us a kind of control over that field; but it may be a kind of control we do not prize very highly. A less learned man may be able to tell us less, but what he has to tell may be more useful to us, because more suited to our needs or wants, and so give us what is in some respects less control over a field, but a more valuable sort of control.

A good bibliographical consultant is one who is able to give good advice about a certain body of writings. No consultant will be expected to replace all bibliographical instruments, for no one can be expected to remember all or a majority of the writings in his field of competence.[1] But a good consultant might be able to say whether those writings were likely to contain anything, or much, of value for this or that purpose, and to be able to suggest the most direct ways of locating and identifying what was of value. A good adviser would be able to say where to start, and whether starting was worthwhile, whether one might expect to find much or little of value and where one might expect to find it. He would be able to understand our purposes, and make reasonable suggestions, if not specific recommendations, about the best ways of attaining them; but he might also suggest that our purpose was unattainable, or that no textual means would be likely to be of much value.

There are plenty of things one might try to do by first reading a book, which no amount of reading will help one do; one of the offices of the consultant is to point those cases out. It must not be thought that only the very ignorant man can profitably use the services of a bibliographical consultant.

---

[1] But a good adviser can in fact be expected to remember the most important writings. This needs no argument; but it is not out of place to quote Jesse H. Shera, *Historians, Books, and Libraries* (Cleveland, 1953), p. 97: "expertly selective recommendations are likely to be the cream of the relevant literature." Shera claims to have got about a quarter of his bibliography for a history from correspondence and communication from others, and a most important quarter.

No matter how learned a person is, he may pose bibliographical questions which are, simply, stupid; they have no answer, they do not even make sense. A person who seeks bibliographical aid in the solution of some problem may be looking for what does not and even could not exist, which facts the consultant might be able to inform him of. The consultant may know that a given sort of question has never been answered, that it may have been answered but that there is little chance of finding the answer, that the answer would not have the value the questioner thinks it would have. A good consultant, in bibliographical as in other matters, warns us of our own folly and ignorance.

In this the consultant is to be distinguished from the bibliographical *aid*. An aid is, we shall say, one who can discover for us the answers to bibliographical questions if the answers can be got immediately or mediately from bibliographical instruments, in the senses of "immediate" and "mediate" explained earlier. He is one who can do those things which can be done on the basis of knowledge of the specifications of bibliographical instruments, a minimum of general knowledge, and the specific instructions of the person he is aiding. This is a deliberately narrow account of the capabilities of a bibliographical aid; wider accounts can be supplied at will. But the contrast intended is that between one who can claim no knowledge of the values and utilities of writings, nor any such knowledge as would make him an expert hunter (as described earlier), and one who can properly claim to be able to give advice, on the basis of knowledge which would also and incidentally make him a potentially better hunter than others.

An aid might know much more about the available bibliographical instruments and their Specifications than the consultant, and be able to make uses of them that the consultant could not make (for example, using bibliographies printed in unfamiliar scripts); but if his uses were such as did not require the knowledge necessary for good hunting and picking, his ability could be described as "purely technical," and his uses "merely routine." This is the sort of ability expected of trained librarians, who are not either expected or in some cases even allowed to give advice other than that advice that depends solely on a knowledge of bibliographical instruments.[2] Of

---

[2] Obviously a dangerous and incendiary claim! But so much is, I think, undeniable: it is not a condition of receiving a professional degree that one be able to give good or reasonable advice about reading in any field of writings whatever. A person may receive a degree in librarianship who knows nothing about anything except the "tools of the trade," if he has managed to get good enough marks in some acceptable college. One may require to know something other than the "tools of the trade" to qualify as a "reader's adviser," but that is a particular specialty within the profession.

course there is no sharp line dividing those capable of giving advice and making the more demanding uses of bibliographical instruments from those capable only of the simpler routine work of the bibliographical aid. The difference between consultant and aid rests on the differences in the things people can be trusted to do, know how to do, and in what their opinions are worth; these things are all matters of more or less, and the good bibliographical consultant and the bibliographical aid are just typical figures which particular individuals more or less resemble.

But if people cannot be sorted out nicely into consultants and aids, still the difference between the two *types* is clear and striking; no number of people who can be trusted only or primarily to carry out routine activities is equivalent to one good adviser, as no number of people who can tie a bandage skillfully is equivalent to one good diagnostician. The most striking difference lies perhaps in this: the bibliographical aid might be set the task of carrying out a search for all writings fitting some description he could apply, a task the consultant could immediately see to be a stupid one, while the aid was quite unaware of its stupidity. The use of bibliographical instruments is frequently a stupid activity, as is, I suspect, known more or less clearly to many scholars, and provides an excellent reason why they should not do more of it. The bibliographical aid, lacking the knowledge necessary to interpret clues and locate the best hunting grounds, cannot be expected even to make the most successful use of instruments whose characteristics he knows well; but even if he does as well as can be done, he is in no position to recognize the foolishness of doing what he is set to do.

There are many ways in which a person comes to have the knowledge of a field of writings necessary to his being a good bibliographical consultant: his apprentice training, his later study and work, particularly as they involve continued exposure to parts of the formal and informal bibliographical apparatus, his participation in keeping up that apparatus. One who reviews the work of others for publication, or who helps in the making of abstracting journals or periodically published bibliographies, adds by those activities to his own stock of bibliographical knowledge.

Of course there are ways other than these obvious ones, of which the most important, in some cases at least, may be one's forming the focal point of many bibliographical *groups*. A number of people who are in the habit of exchanging opinions and information about writings may be said to constitute a bibliographical group. The opinions and information exchanged need not be novel nor concern what is new. The group need not be formally organized; it need have no set apparatus of exchange, no rules or formal procedures. The habit of exchange need not mean constant or frequent exchange, it might even be only a generally dormant readiness or disposition to exchange opinion and information, a recognition by each of all the others as being receptive of opinion and information, and able and willing to reciprocate. A literary intelligentsia such as those of Paris or London or New York constitutes a group, or many interlocking groups, the members of which are bound together by interest in works of literature, of politics, and of a vaguely defined peripheral set of topics clustered around the core of literature and politics.

The group is interested in discovering new writings of value, reevaluating and interpreting the old writings recognized as being of central importance, propagandizing on behalf of and educating in the "true" value of the old and the new. Such a group may be expected to have leaders and followers, insiders and marginal members, full- and part-time members, members specialized in function as educators, commentators, synthesizers, popularizers, discoverers, even rebels and professional denigrators. The circulation of information within such groups, and from group to group, and the molding of opinion that constantly goes on in such groups, are topics within the province of the sociologist, whose job is to describe as accurately as possible how such groups "work," how they come into existence, what goes on in them, at what rate of speed and under what impetus. The sociologist may give an exacter picture than we could otherwise get of the circulation of information and opinion within and between groups;[3] but we have only to reflect on our own experience to see how important personal exchanges are or can be in adding to our stock of knowledge and opinion of writings, as of everything else.

The most important bibliographical groups are, for our purposes, those

---

[3] There is a large and fast-growing literature on the "scientific communication system," the "totality of all publications, facilities, occasions, institutional arrangements, and customs which affect the direct or indirect transmission of scientific messages among scientists."— Herbert Menzel, "Planned and Unplanned Scientific Communication," *Proceedings of the International Conference on Scientific Information, Washington, D.C., 1958*, I, 201. A fairly good summary of work to 1960 is the *Review of Studies in the Flow of Information Among Scientists*, prepared for the National Science Foundation by the Bureau of Applied Social Research (Columbia University, 1960). An outstanding example of more recent work is *Reports of the American Psychological Association's Project on Scientific Information Exchange in Psychology*, I (Washington, D.C., 1963). Menzel's article cited above is very good. So is Melvin J. Voigt, *Scientists' Approaches to Information*, ACRL Monograph no. 24 (Chicago, 1961). And see Derek J. de Solla Price's chapter on "Invisible Colleges and the Affluent Scientific Commuter," in his *Little Science, Big Science* (New York, 1965), pp. 62–91.

whose members have in common a métier, in the general sense of occupation, trade, profession: those engaged in the same line of work. Being in the same line of work constitutes a strong bond, and while the members of a métier do not automatically constitute a bibliographical group, it is immediately intelligible that such a group or such groups should grow up among the membership of a métier. Writings are of unequal importance in different jobs; between the philologist who lives on texts and the barber or shepherd lies a great gulf separating the completely literature-bound from the almost or entirely literature-free. Even among those who live for and on writings, a man can work in independence of others and rely for his knowledge of writings solely on his independent discoveries; but it is natural that the more important writings are to the practitioners of a métier, the more likely we are to find a proliferation of bibliographical groups.

Bibliographical information is not the only sort of information that practitioners of a métier are wont to exchange, and we may expect that bibliographical groups will be identical in membership with groups defined in terms of other sorts of informational exchange. And opinions about the value of writings are not the only opinions that circulate and are gradually formed among men in a line of work, so we may expect that bibliographical reputation-building groups will be identical in membership with opinion-making groups defined in other than bibliographic terms. Still it is useful to consider bibliographical groups as if clearly distinct from other sorts of groups, and to consider in a bit more detail the sort of exchange of information and opinion likely to take place. News of the writings of one's fellow workers will be circulated, in virtue either of personal interest or simply an interest in the progress of the métier as such. Other practitioners are one's fellows, engaged in a common enterprise, and news of the work of one's fellows is naturally of interest, and naturally discussed. That this should happen really needs no explanation; what would need explanation would be a lack of interest among practitioners of a métier in what other practitioners were doing.

If one thinks of the group as having as a common enterprise the adding to the body of knowledge, or attempting to master some range of phenomena, news will naturally be welcome which tells of additions and successes. But there is a more pointed sort of interest in news. As a merchant wants to know not merely what is going on in the world of trade, but more particularly what other merchants are doing that is likely to affect his own enterprise, so the practitioner of any métier will as a matter of course be interested in knowing what fellow practitioners are doing that bears on his own enterprise. The possible bearings are various. If another has discovered what he thinks is a better procedure for doing what I am engaged in doing, or would be engaged in doing if there were adequate ways of doing it, I will want to know. If another has succeeded in doing something which I am trying to do, I will want to know, for I may (but need not) decide to stop trying, either because there is no alternative way of succeeding, or, if there is, because I think I am unlikely to achieve a greater or equal success, or do not think it sufficiently important to try. Frequently it is supposed that, if I learn that another has succeeded, or claims to have succeeded, at doing something I am trying to do, I will automatically stop; or it is supposed that this is invariably so in scholarly métiers.[4] But it is not invariably so, nor should it be. Only if there is only one way of succeeding, and all that counts is first success, is it necessarily so. Still, I shall want to see what others have done, or at least know of their claims. And in general, I shall want to know of anything done by my colleagues that might help me in doing whatever I am trying to do. And the members of a bibliographical group, knowing each other's interests, will naturally circulate information that feeds those interests.

There is another sort of news that one naturally wants to have, news of the doings of practitioners of other métiers that might affect one's own work. I may have a more or less vague and general interest in what is going on in various parts of the world, but be content with the most diffuse and fragmentary accounts except where my own interests are touched, when I will suddenly demand exact and detailed accounts. If my own work might be helped or hindered by events in other areas, if I suspect that future developments may have harmful or beneficial effects, I shall want to keep the other areas under surveillance, and my expectation of the likelihood and magnitude of such effects will determine, if I am quite rational, the extent of the attention I give to happenings in those areas. If other members of my bibliographical group happen to be members of other métiers than my own, or to be members of other groups including such outsiders, they will natur-

---

[4] It is even supposed that I will never try to do what I know others are trying to do, which is preposterous. "A scholar does not knowingly undertake the solution of a problem which another scholar is already studying," writes Tyrus Hillway, *Introduction to Research* (Boston, 1956), p. 74. Surely the truth is that there are at any time fashionable problems, on which many people are simultaneously working. How many of those interested in information retrieval would stop working at the notion of relevance if they heard that someone else was also working at it? They *know* that many others are doing so.

ally pass on to me what they think I will find worth knowing. This is, again, something so natural as to need no explaining; not only benevolence but malice and a love of gossip lead us to point out to our colleagues and coworkers the happenings and writings in remote fields which we think to have a bearing on what they are doing.[5]

There is a fourth sort of exchange that is of importance. The significance of a man's work, the reputation of the man and his work, are primarily matters for his peers to decide; for although a man may have a wide following and a high reputation among the general public who know and care little about his scientific or professional work, it is recognized and indeed must be recognized that only those engaged in the same line of work as he are fully competent to say how good he is in that line of work. But the judgment of a man's work by his peers is not solely based on solitary calm reflection; it is determined as well by personal exchanges of sentiment or opinion among members of bibliographical groups. The bibliographical consultant comes, by membership in such groups, to learn of, as well as to help in forming, the reputations of other men and other writings, knowledge which plays no unimportant part in his activities as consultant.

A man who actively participates in groups exchanging general news of the progress of the métier, particular news of interest to particular members, foreign news of concern to the group or particular members, and opinions and evaluations about the importance or significance of the work of others, thus adds to his stock of bibliographical information and maintains or improves his ability to serve as bibliographical consultant. Participation in such groups is certainly not the only way in which a person comes by the knowledge that is needed in a good consultant; but it is one way. Acquiring and maintaining mastery over a field of writings is a central task of the scholar, a task that is claimed to be increasingly difficult as the number of writings in existence increases. Evidently the proportion of the total mass of writings that any one man can master decreases as the total mass increases, and the field of competence of consultants diminishes in relative size, and can be expected to continue to diminish. But this only means that more consultants are needed than formerly if one is to have available to him advice about the totality of writings, or some specified field within that totality. However great the proliferation of writings, it cannot be a danger

---

[5] The importance of "foreign news" is perfectly well known, the difficulty or impossibility of getting it from bibliographical instruments, perhaps less well known. On the necessity of interdisciplinary cooperation to assure an adequate supply of such news, see, for instance, Russell L. Ackoff, *The Design of Social Research* (Chicago, 1953), pp. 52–53.

that the time might come when no one could be master of any writings at all.

A directory of bibliographical consultants, not to be identified with either a directory of scholars or a directory of consultants prepared to give other than bibliographical advice, might be considered as furnishing the list of contributors to a Bibliographical Encyclopedia of the sort imagined earlier and contrasted with an imaginary Catalog. The Encyclopedia was an instrument in which utility rather than "subject" furnished the basis for organization, and the particular virtue of the good consultant is his ability to estimate the utilities of writings for various purposes, to recommend suitable textual means to given ends. J. D. Bernal long ago lamented the fact that specialists in different scientific fields were in effect required to become chapters in a bibliographical encylopedia (which he may not have thought of in the way outlined above).[*] But it is not easy to see why one should lament the possession by specialists of the sort of knowledge that makes them good consultants. The value of the consultants goes far beyond their having the knowledge that would make them suitable contributors to a Bibliographical Encyclopedia, or "chapters" of an ambulatory encyclopedia. They might write down their contributions, but they know more than they could ever write down.

No bibliographical instrument could be made which was equally aimed at, and equally suitable to the situations of, all its potential users; but no matter how large an instrument was made, no matter how many interests and situations were foreseen, there would remain over some interests and situations unforeseen, to which the consultants could address themselves if they were presented with them. They may know more than they realize, for it may be only on the occasion of a question that they see or realize applications and utilities of writings with which they are perfectly familiar.

---

[*] J. D. Bernal, *The Social Function of Science* (London, 1939), p. 264: "To a large extent the specialist's isolation is due to the fact that he and he alone really knows the literature of the subject, not because the literature is particularly incomprehensible, but because it is presented in such a maze of papers without adequate summaries or critical reports that the outside scientist might spend months in finding his way through it. Consequently the specialist is needed as a kind of living encyclopaedia, or rather as one article in such an encyclopaedia, which, it should be realized, is a terrible waste of human personality." The conclusion is curious; does Bernal mean to suggest that the specialist should not be a master of the literature of his specialty? or that he should not waste his time telling others what they should read? or that he should not have to remember anything of what he has previously read? No doubt it is desirable that the literature of a subject not be a maze, but Bernal seems to claim that the waste of personality lies in the specialist's *being*, not in his laboriously *becoming*, a chapter in a living encyclopedia, and that claim is at the least obscure.

It is the peculiar human ability to *re*-organize and *re*-describe and *re*-evaluate from novel points of view that makes for the superiority of the consultants over any set of bibliographical instruments, as well as the human ability to recognize a question as misconceived or stupid.

The virtues of instruments as against human memory are simply their greater capacity for preserving indefinitely a huge mass of detail. Bibliographical instruments might in fact be seen as simply *aides-mémoire* to the consultant, public memories. But these public memories are rigid in organization and inflexible in description; they do not respond to questions, or only in limited and rigidly defined ways, and cannot reevaluate their own contents. We can easily imagine devices by which a public memory could within modest limits reorganize itself on demand; a catalog, or some analogous instrument, could be devised that would on request display its contents in several different arrangements. But the possible alternate arrangements must be unambiguously specified by the human constructor of the catalog when it is put together, and thereafter it cannot, without further human intervention, do other than mechanically go through its limited variety of tricks.

A human being, on the other hand, can reconsider his stock of knowledge and opinion in terms of a completely novel concept, or a completely novel requirement. He may not in fact manage to produce what meets the requirement, even when something he knows about would meet the requirement; but that is simply a failure in a sort of performance in which he is at least sometimes capable of success, while no instrument is ever capable of it at all.[7]

---

[7] It may be argued that such distinctions between what machines can do and what only humans can do are of merely temporary interest, since in principle there is nothing that a human can do that a machine might not be devised, some day, to do. Whatever the force of this metaphysical claim, it is clear enough that, for the foreseeable future, bibliographical consultants will be able to do things that no bibliographical machines can do. I shall not attempt to suggest readings in the literature on "artificial intelligence," and of the more or less philosophical literature on the possibility of a "thinking machine," I shall mention only the lucid and witty essay of A. M. Turing, "Computing Machinery and Intelligence," *Mind*, 59 (1950), 433–460.

CHAPTER VIII

RELIABILITY

RECOGNITION of the distinction between giving advice and giving aid, between Bibliographical Consultant and Bibliographical Aid, need not be accompanied by ability to apply the distinction in practice, to identify those who deserve the title of Consultant and separate them from those who can only claim the status of Aid. How would we discover or establish the reliability or trustworthiness of one who offered bibliographical advice? Would it be by counting his successes, the proportion of cases in which the advice offered was good, or very good, or the best possible? But how do we recognize the successes? Other sorts of consultants give advice of the kind that may lead to results we can definitely identify as successes or failures. An engineering consultant whose clients' bridges and skyscrapers always fell down would soon lose his commissions and contracts; a medical consultant whose advice was always followed by the patient's death would soon cease to be consulted. The medical consultant's successes are, I suppose, those cases in which the patient recovers against all expectation, and the engineer's advice will be counted excellent if his clients' bridges and skyscrapers withstand earthquakes and hurricanes; but where is the analogue in the case of bibliographical advice?

No doubt there are cases in which the goodness of advice can be simply and directly discovered: cases in which we are advised to look in one place rather than another for some bit of information, or in which we are warned that few writings of a given sort will be discovered in such and such an instrument, may present no difficulty when we set out to evaluate the advice given. Even in such simple cases, however, good advice cannot be simply identified as that which leads to success, nor bad advice as that which leads to failure, since the most reasonable course of action may not lead to the desired outcome, just as the most probable event may not occur, and in any case success may depend on good performance in following the advice given, as well as on the quality of the advice. More important, however, is the fact that the marks of success and failure are not always evident or indisputable, and the further fact that the very notions of success and failure are not everywhere applicable. If an adviser whom I already trust tells me that I should find such and such a writing logically relevant to the hypotheses or arguments of my work, I shall try to see it as such, and may manage to do so, which result would count as a "success" if the writing actually had any such relevance; but logical relevance is far from being a characteristic we can simply detect on inspection of a writing, and other advisers and critics may call the writing irrelevant and the advice not just poor but pernicious. If my adviser tells me that a certain work is worth examining, and I do look at it but find nothing in it to my purpose, the outcome is perhaps no success but neither is it a "failure" (except, perhaps, on my part), and does nothing at all to discredit the advice. The outcomes of following advice are not simply divisible into successes and failures; nor is there any necessary unanimity on how those that can be described as success or failure should be assigned to either category.

To admit that the notions of success and failure are not everywhere applicable is not, of course, to claim that advice cannot be evaluated; and to admit that unanimity cannot be expected on the question whether a given outcome is a success or a failure is not to claim that every opinion is equally valuable. But who is competent to evaluate advice, and whose opinions about success and failure deserve to be taken seriously? The same air of paradox attends the problem of evaluating an adviser, or of choosing among advisers, as attends the problem of evaluating a teacher, or choosing among teachers. If we know as much as those who offer their services, we do not need those services; but if we need their services, we do not know enough to choose the best adviser or teacher. If we think we know as much as an adviser, we will claim the competence to judge the quality of the advice he gives; but if we do not know as much as he, how can we judge? Of course we might appeal to external marks of professional success: many publications, many government contracts, many speaking engagements. But in our lucid moments we distrust these marks. We may appeal to the reputation a man has among his fellow workers, saying that *they* must be able to distinguish good advice from bad if anyone can. But their opinions will not usually be unanimous, and in any case are not unchangeable. If a man's co-workers reject him as foolish or eccentric, they may still at a later time reverse their verdict and blame themselves for misunderstanding or shortsightedness. We may, finally, be content with an appeal to the satisfaction felt by the recipients of advice. Not attempting to distinguish justified from unjustified sentiments of satisfaction, we might simply count cases of satisfaction and dissatisfaction. But it is hard to believe that satisfied clients prove a good adviser, in this any more than in other areas of life. The ques-

Reliability

tion can always be asked, though it cannot always be answered, whether the satisfaction that was felt was actually warranted.

If attempts to evaluate advice, and estimate the reliability of consultants, are likely to lack precise and unequivocal outcomes, attempts to evaluate, and estimate the reliability of, bibliographical instruments might seem by comparison a satisfactory objective and straightforward affair. We cannot know how much power is made available to us by a bibliographical instrument unless we know both the plan or Specifications of the work and the quality of the workmanship.[1] And each of the separate elements of the Specifications offers a field for the evaluation of performance. Has the domain been considered with sufficient care? Have the selection principles been applied consistently and judiciously? Have the units to be separately listed been chosen correctly and consistently? Has the description and evaluation called for been done accurately and soundly? Has assignment to positions been done correctly? If all these questions are affirmatively answered, the work can then be pronounced reliable or trustworthy: what it claims to do, it does, and what it tries to do well, it succeeds in doing well. The overall reliability or trustworthiness of an instrument depends in part on the exactness and accuracy and consistency with which the rules embodied in the Specifications are applied, in part on the soundness of scholarship and judgment exhibited, when scholarship and judgment rather than the mechanical application of rules are what is called for. Where the rules can be said to determine unambiguously what is to be done in a particular case, we hope the worker will have recognized the applicability of the appropriate rule, and followed it. Where the rules require decision and evaluation, we hope the decision will be sensible and the evaluation sound.

This is easily said, but not easily done, nor easily recognized when done.

---

[1] It would clearly be desirable always to be able to test the reliability of a work independently of discovering the Specifications of the work, for it is only by reference to a particular set of Specifications that reliability can be judged. Unfortunately this often cannot be done. If the Specifications are announced, still they may not have been adhered to, and some other unannounced Specifications followed instead. If they are not announced, we must make hypotheses about them, and try the hypotheses out; in such testing, however, we must simultaneously test reliability. We cannot test reliability except on the basis of some hypotheses or other about Specifications, for there is no such thing as a failure or a success except in relation to some plan being pursued. But in order to test an hypothesis about Specifications, we must assess the reliability of the work viewed as constructed according to the imagined Specifications; the best supported hypothesis is that according to which the work turns out most reliable. What is most untrustworthy, viewed in the light of one imagined set of Specifications, may be perfectly trustworthy, viewed as an attempt to follow another set; what is a failure, taken as an attempt to do one sort of thing, may be a success as an attempt to do another sort of thing.

A bibliography might, for instance, claim to be complete for a given subject, to list the entire literature of that subject. It is a commonplace that such claims are seldom correct, since no bibliographer, however diligent, can hope to avoid "missing" items required for completeness. But can we indeed be certain what is required for completeness? Behind the commonplaces lies the assumption that it should in principle be possible to divide the totality of writings into two natural groups, those that belong to the literature of a given subject, and the rest. But there is no apparent reason why this should be; it is much more plausible to think that "the literature" of a subject consists of a core of central writings surrounded by an indefinitely large group of more or less peripheral writings, yet without boundaries anywhere. If this is so, how does one treat claims to completeness, or evaluate the selection of items in a bibliography? Or suppose the claim made, in a bibliography, to list every edition of every text of some very well know work; if the discussion above[2] is even approximately correct, there must be cases in which such a claim to completeness could neither be substantiated nor refuted, simply because there is no recipe by which membership of given texts in the "family" of texts constituting a work can invariably be determined. But questions of completeness are not the only ones that promise to make difficult the evaluation of performance. In the light of our earlier discussion of the notion of the subject of a writing, the question of the correctness of assignments to positions in an organizational scheme can scarcely appear an easy one to answer.[3] Nor does the evaluation of indexing, as that term was earlier used, promise to be easy or uncontroversial, if the criteria for choice of assignments are, as earlier argued, not completely specifiable.[4]

Clearly there are parts and features of bibliographical instruments that can be evaluated in direct and uncontroversial ways. If we know for in-

---

[2] See above, pages 10–11.

[3] It is always good fun to find what one takes to be obvious mistakes in, for example, the printed subject catalog of the Library of Congress; how is it possible that, for instance, a book such as *Frontiers of Knowledge in the Study of Man*, ed. Lynn White Jr. (New York, 1956), be assigned the single heading "Anthropology—Addresses, Essays, Lectures"? It contains chapters on genetics, psychology, cultural anthropology, archaeology, history, sociology, politics, geography, economics, history of science, musicology, art history, literature, linguistics, mathematics, philosophy, and religion. Is it that "anthropology" means, to the catalogers of the Library of Congress, simply the study of man in general and all his works? Our ignorance of the Specifications of that subject catalog forbids us to call this a simple mistake. The example is taken at random; anyone who tries can find dozens of equally inexplicable things.

[4] See the first part of Chapter VI above.

stance what rules of description were employed in the construction of an instrument, we may be able to tell whether they have been followed consistently and accurately in a quite mechanical fashion. Other parts and features we will be able to evaluate properly only if we have ourselves the good sense and judgment that we hope the worker will have exhibited. Wherever, for instance, judgments of importance have to be made by the worker, whether in selecting items from the domain, deciding on what to mention in a description of contents, or deciding on the number of positions to be assigned, we can evaluate his performance only by employing our own putative good sense, by asking whether what the worker did is what we would have done, or is at least one of the alternatives we would have thought admissible. Evidently, so far as judgments of reliability must be based on one's notions of what good sense requires, such judgments will be as various and conflicting as are those notions. We cannot hope to arrive at universally acceptable gradings of bibliographical instruments according to reliability, any more than we could hope to arrive at universally acceptable gradings of judges or teachers according to wisdom or good sense.

That conclusion will be admitted, no doubt, for those bibliographical instruments that announce themselves as "selective" and "evaluative"; what must be insisted upon is that the number of bibliographical instruments that require no judgment in their construction, only painstaking accuracy in the performance of mechanical operations, is an insignificant one.[5] Selection, evaluation, decision not dictated by exact rule, are everywhere the rule rather than the exception. The flaws we detect in bibliographical instruments are by no means all "mistakes," violations of explicit rule; they are as frequently what we think to be flaws of judgment, or exhibitions of less than perfectly good sense. But flaws of judgment cannot be recognized except by persons of good judgment; the criticism of bibliographical instruments is as little a matter of mechanical routine as their construction.

There is another place at which estimates of reliability must be made.

---

[5] I am not in this section speaking of the *design* of an instrument, that is, the drawing up of Specifications, but of the workmanship displayed in following the Specifications. The "insignificant number" spoken of may not remain insignificant, as bibliographical information stored in forms convenient for automatic processing is recast in the form of "bibliographies" of one sort or another. It should be noted that if a computer produces a bibliography by manipulation of a store of bibliographic data, it does so not by selecting items fitting a given description, but by identifying items to which particular descriptive labels have been previously assigned; this is the sort of "superficial" bibliography-making practiced by bibliographical aids who can recognize labels that others have attached to descriptions of writings, but not tell whether the labels fit.

No matter how reliable an instrument may be, those who use it may use it well or badly. If hunting or picking is required, it may be done skillfully or ineptly; even when neither of these is required, the user may, through carelessness or ignorance of the Specifications or failure to see relationships between his way, and other possible ways, of describing that which he seeks, fail to use the instrument as well as he might. Of several men using the same instrument for the same or similar purposes, one might have occasional brilliant successes and frequent disastrous failures, another might regularly attain mediocre results, another might have a monotonous series of triumphs, the differences in regularity of achievement of a particular level of success being attributable to the skill, care, and knowledge of the different men. It is unnecessary to repeat the considerations which argue the difficulty of recognizing successes and failures. It should also be unnecessary to argue, what seems obvious enough, that the degree of bibliographical control a man actually wields cannot simply be measured by considering the instruments available to him, but depends on his ability to make good use of those instruments. The characteristics of the available instruments and consultants set a limit to what is discoverable, the abilities and knowledge of the user set a limit to what will be discovered.

If we consider the range of bibliographical questions that could be answered, entirely or in part, imperfectly or perfectly, by the best possible use of all the bibliographical apparatus and arrangements available to a man, we can form an idea, vague though it be, of the reliability of power in one sense available to that man; if we measure his abilities, or the abilities of his aids, against the abilities requisite for the best possible use of the apparatus and arrangements, we can form an idea of the actual reliability of his power. By examination of the apparatus we might discover that complete answers to one type of question were generally available, that is, could be found by the best use of the apparatus; by examination of the man, we might conclude that *he* is likely to find only partial answers to questions of that type, if and when he ever tries. We may discover what can be done on the basis of a judicious choice among bibliographical instruments, but also conclude that he is unlikely to make judicious choices among instruments. But such attempts to estimate the overall reliability of his power, the regularity with which he can command or carry out performances with a given degree of success, cannot be expected to have precise, quantitative conclusions. Estimating the overall reliability of this sort of power is not to be compared with, say, the situation of the technician trying the performance of an automobile under a variety of test conditions, to see what it is capable of; it is rather to be compared, for instance, with that of a general, attempting to predict what his troops will do under various not yet encountered circumstances, with the equipment at their disposal, and on various hypotheses about his own performance in the choice of plans, and the selection of subordinates to excute them. Though the general can come to a rough but fair estimate of how much can generally be expected of his men, in a given range of circumstances, it would be foolish to hope for any exact, quantitative statement of just how reliable they are.

An estimate of power is an estimate of what one could do if one tried, of what success would be achieved in different attempts. The existence of multitudes of cases in which success cannot be recognized with certainty, or in which the very notion of success is of doubtful applicability, added to the obvious difficulties of estimating a power on the basis of a sample set of trials, effectively prevent such estimates, in the bibliographical case, from claiming exactitude or finality. The reliability of our power over writings, like the reliability of our power over the circumstances of our daily lives, can only be precariously and roughly estimated.

CHAPTER IX

ADEQUACY AND BIBLIOGRAPHICAL POLICY

LET US IMAGINE a Supreme Bibliographical Council, whose task it was to evaluate the bibliographical situations of individuals and groups of individuals, to estimate the degree of bibliographical control available to them, to decide on its adequacy or inadequacy, and to suggest or order changes in those situations, by the creation of new bibliographical instruments or new institutional arrangements, or by the alteration of old arrangements, or by making more widely available instruments and services hitherto restricted in availability. Their business, we will suppose, would be to hear complaints from individuals and groups, and to consider the reports of their staff of bibliographical examiners, who would undertake their own appraisals of the situations of the complainants and also of non-complainants.

At a typical sitting the Council might for instance hear complaints from the professional association of students of extra-sensory-perception that there was no abstracting service available to their group, from some historians of science that the principal bibliographies available to them were inadequately indexed, from some "area specialists" that Nepalese publications were almost unobtainable outside Nepal, from some teachers of genetics that there were too few and inadequate reviews of progress in genetics. The sorts of complaints that might be received are familiar enough: delays in publication, delays in communication of news to interested parties, insufficient and inadequate abstracts and indexes, no cumulations of periodically published bibliographies and indexes, lack of bibliographical coverage of possibly important classes of publications, lack of bibliographical services specifically devoted to the interests of a particular group, inconsistencies and other inadequacies in bibliographical services, and many other grievances.[1]

But in addition to complaints from those whose situation is less satisfactory than they would like it to be and think it should be, and who are accustomed to making their dissatisfactions publicly known, there might

---

[1] Any discussion of the bibliographical situation in a subject field will afford examples of the different sorts of complaints. The Royal Society's Scientific Information Conference *Report* (London, 1948), is an excellent source for the typology of complaints. There is useful material in Paule Salvan, *Les Lacunes des Bibliographies Internationales Specialisées* (Paris, 1953). Two recent issues of *Library Trends*, 15, Nos. 3–4 (1967) are devoted to brief reviews of the state of bibliography in different fields and for different types of publication.

also be reports from the examiners on the lamentable bibliographical ignorance of some groups of people, who have more power than they realize or ever exercise, and on the dismal situation of other groups who have little power but also are unaccustomed to complain publicly about their little power. The examiner would point out that the situation of the uncomplaining was as bad as, or worse than, that of the complaining; the Council would have to decide whose situation required or deserved amelioration, what were the most suitable methods of ameliorating the situation, and what the order of priority was to be among different demands for assistance. How would, or could, they decide these things?

We can well imagine that a Supreme Bibliographical Council might make its decisions on a purely ad hoc basis, judging each case "on its merits," trying without any general principles or policies to do "justice" to the conflicting contenders for patronage. But let us try to imagine what general principles or policies might be proposed to guide their decisions, and see what might be said for or against them. Let us start with this statement by an eminent American librarian and student of librarianship, E. C. Richardson:

> The fundamental object of bibliography is to enable a thinker to get together the results of previous thinkers on the same subject in order to build on this foundation, avoiding the labor of repeating work already done—not to mention the humiliation of finding when the work has really been finished that it has been done before and perhaps done better.[2]

What is said here is familiar enough, representing a constantly reiterated claim about the aims of bibliography and indeed about education in general. Only the barbarian or the fool supposes himself to be the first man ever to have been faced with a problem of a given sort, or ever to have thought or wondered about some feature of the world; one of the aims of education is to make us aware when young of how much has already been thought and done, and teach us to build consciously on the best available foundations. The aim of bibliography is that of allowing us to discover what exactly has been thought and done, what foundations are available. And if that is indeed *the* aim of bibliography, then the major

---

[2] Ernest Cushing Richardson, "The Bibliography of the War and the Reconstruction of Bibliographical Methods," *Papers of the Bibliographical Society of America*, 13 (1919), 113. S. C. Bradford, in his *Documentation* (London, 1948), p. 11, explains documentation as the process by which is "put before the creative specialist the existing literature, bearing on the subject of his investigation, in order that he may be made fully aware of previous achievements in his subject, and thus be saved from the dissipation of his genius upon work already done."

lines of a general bibliographical policy are clear: one's decisions on particular cases must be made in the light of that aim.

But is the aim so clear? or the statement of aim unexceptionable? Consider the word "results": the aim is said to be that of getting together previous results. Unhappily the word is ambiguous as between what a man discovers and what he thinks he discovers, what he proves and what he supposes himself to prove, what he explains and what he supposes himself to have explained. Of course it is frequently, though by no means always, a waste of time proving what has already been proved, discovering what has already been discovered, explaining what has already been explained. But it is not always a waste of time *trying* to prove what others have tried and failed to prove, and not even necessarily a waste of time trying to prove it in the very ways in which they tried unsuccessfully; and analogously for activities other than proving.

Now shall we say that the object of bibliography is to enable a thinker to get together the results of earlier thinkers, in the sense of actual proofs, explanations, discoveries, or shall we want it possible also to get together the failures as well as the successes? Let us suppose the latter, for failures can be as instructive as successes. But then, what of records of previous work that led to no results at all, no real or claimed successes? Shall we forget about them simply because they do not report any discovery which we might, through ignorance, wastefully rediscover? But work which leads to no results may yet be written about, and what is said may be helpful to one now setting out on the same or a similar course of work. This talk of "results" repellently suggests that we cannot afford to lose sight of any supposedly real discovery, proof, explanation, however tiny, but that we can afford to forget, or assign to an inferior category, writings that contain no such "results."

Even if it were acceptable to assign highest priority to ensuring the ability to collect "results," in those fields in which it makes sense to speak of results, still it has to be recognized that there are fields in which it makes no such sense to talk of results. It would be slightly absurd to approach the study of literary criticism, or metaphysics, or theology, or political theory, or historiography, with the aim of first digesting the results of earlier studies, in order to avoid doing over what had already been done, proving what had been proved, explaining what had already been explained, discovering what had already been discovered. To suppose that the problem of the freedom of the will might already have been solved, or the value of Pope's poetry determined, or the optimum form of political or social organization discovered, or the nature of consciousness established, so that one was in danger of wasting one's time by doing over what had already been done, is to betray ignorance of the nature of those questions and problems. Certainly if one works in ignorance of what others have already written on these and a thousand other topics, one may waste one's time; but that is not because, seeing what others have written, one sees what has been proved or discovered and so needs no further discussion.

Nor is it because a thing once done need not be done over; rather, it can be argued that the things once done have to be done over again and again, by each man as he struggles to understand what others have thought they understood, following routes they pointed out. We do not read Aristotle or Aquinas or even William James for their "results," but for what they say that may illumine us, for what we might not else have thought of, or what might have taken us painful years to think out for ourselves. But then we do not simply note what they say and pass on to new topics, for we have to persuade ourselves of the truth or falsity of what they say, which requires doing over what they have done. It is only by doing over for ourselves what others have done that we can come to have what can be called reasoned opinions.

No doubt this is to take too seriously the use of the word "results" in the statement of the aim of bibliography quoted above; perhaps we should have interpreted it to mean, the written products of study or thought, so that whatever a man wrote down about the freedom of the will or the best form of political or social organization after or while thinking about those topics would be called his "results." Suppose we reconstrue the quotation to mean that the aim of bibliography is to enable a thinker to get together what others have written on the same subject, in order to build on that foundation, not necessarily just to avoid repeating work already done, but simply so that he will be in the best possible starting position, and will not be liable to repeat others' work unwittingly. To know, or be able to discover, everything that has previously been written on the subject one proposes to study, is a necessary prelude to the most reasonable and efficient study; and one is in the best starting position when one can play that prelude. So the, or a primary, aim of bibliographical policy would be to make it possible to get together all the writings in existence on any topic.

If it seems a much too limited aim, merely to provide means of collecting all the "results" in the senses earlier mentioned of work at any subject, this more generous aim may seem objectionable in another way. Georg Schneider appears to have been delighted rather than disgusted with a bibliography listing every discoverable mention of the island of Capri;[3] but contrast the reaction of the historian Langlois to the notion of a universal subject catalog, which would have claimed to allow collecting all the writings on any topic:[4]

> Sous la rubrique 'Dante,' le Catalogue universel fournira le relevé de 20 à 30 000 articles bibliographiques dont les titres renferment le mot 'Dante,' indiquant (ou paraissent indiquer) qu'il est question de Dante. Mais le Catalogue universel, fait avec des ciseaux, ne distinguera pas ceux de ces articles qui n'ont plus ou qui n'ont jamais eu aucune valeur de ceux qui dispenseraient d'en lire cent.... Vingt mille fiches sur Dante, sans avertissements et sans détails? Il n'y a rien qui soit plus propre à aggraver ces sentiments d'embarras, d'accablement et de paralysie que la surabondance souvent stérile de la littérature contemporaine détermine chez les gens scrupuleux, et que le rôle naturel des instruments bibliographiques est justement de dissiper ou, tout au moins, d'atténuer.

That Langlois was considering a proposal merely to amalgamate all existing catalogs and indexes without examination of the writings there listed does not destroy the force of his objection, for the most scrupulously made catalog of writings that indicates merely "the subject" of each writing and does not distinguish good from bad is equally subject to his sharp complaint. His objections were still more caustic against the proposal of an instrument that would record every crumb of discussion of any topic, that would "analyze" in great detail; nor can there be doubt of the justice of the objections, for what could one do with, not a list of twenty thousand books and articles "on the subject" of Dante, but a list of a million or two of brief discussions and mentions of Dante? Are any of the things one might do with such a list worth doing? Even if they are worth doing, are they so much worth doing as to justify making the

---

[3] Georg Schneider, *Handbuch der Bibliographie* (Leipzig, 1923), p. 52 fn. Others would share his approval. In S. R. Ranganathan's *Classification and Communication* (Delhi, 1951), p. 113, we read: "Why does a librarian classify at all? Why should he practice depth-classification? He classifies and should practice depth-classification to uncover to himself, in order to make it readily available to the appropriate reader, everything, however minute, which the library has on anything—all the micro-units of thought which have been expressed and embodied."

[4] Ch. V. Langlois, *Manuel de Bibliographie Historique*, t. 1 (Paris, 1901), p. 8.

Adequacy and Bibliographical Policy 137

principal aim of a bibliographical policy that of providing the means of collecting all discussions of any topic? Even if that were not claimed as the principal aim, is it even a subsidiary aim?[5]

Consider what use might be made of a list of, say, all discoverable discussions of the freedom of the will. We need not suppose, for it is surely false, that it would be easy to decide which discussions were discussions of that topic; but let us put aside that difficulty. We also put aside the consideration that a list of writings on the freedom of the will is not identical with a list of writings containing material relevant to the problem or question of the freedom of the will, and so would not contain all the writings a student of that problem would profit from reading. Now let us ask what is to be done with this list, which does not contain all of what a student needs, and contains a vast amount of what is surely of no value whatever. If the list does not mark items as important or unimportant, or at least as having been considered by one person or another to be important or unimportant, it is of no value to the man who wants to know what he should read about the freedom of the will, while if it does mark them so, the important ones might better be listed separately and the rest forgotten. But may there not be those who want to know if some person, say Lenin or Saint Theresa, had anything to say about the freedom of the will? There is some use for concordances, after all, and this list might be constructed as a sort of concordance, of limited range, to all writings. And are there not historians, of philosophy and of "ideas," who may care to know the entire course of this fragment of intellectual history? The historian is not interested simply in knowing what philosophically important discussions there have been of the freedom of the

---

[5] Roy Stokes, in his *Bibliographical Control and Service* (London, 1965), p. 46: "The librarian needs to think of the easy efficiency with which a really first-class index opens up the whole of the subject matter of a book. What he needs to consider is that if every book was really fully indexed and if all those indexes were combined, then this is precisely the kind of 'catalogue' which a librarian needs." But for what purpose does the librarian need this impossible monster? "It is always the material which lurks in unexpected places which causes the difficulty," Stokes continues; he mentions a book containing menus of elaborate nineteenth-century dinners, and asks "In how many libraries will this unexpected piece of information be recorded? It is certainly not indexed in the book itself; yet it is precisely the kind of query which could lead to hours of search" (p. 47). I wonder if Stokes would propose the re-indexing of all books, and compilation of one vast master-index, in order to facilitate searches for menus, as a major aim of a general bibliographical policy. For most other purposes, Langlois' remarks quoted above apply; this master-index would cause only "sentiments d'embarras, d'accablement et de paralysie."

will; it is his business to discover what was of historical importance, a discovery he cannot expect others to make for him, but which he might hope to make if he had a list of all the possibly important items.

There is another sort of use that might be expected to be made; Richardson himself describes it:[6]

> This object [of getting together all "results" on a given topic] finds its most definite illustration in the modern university thesis, where the first search is for some topic on which no one else has done anything. Here the actual search is negative; it aims to find some minute subject on which nothing at all has been written. It soon becomes positive, however, in the fact that the process involves the exhaustive gathering of the literature of the entire narrow field in which this special untreated topic or aspect lies.

So the apprentice scholar is expected to gather everything that has been written on some minute topic, and if that topic lies within the larger topic of the freedom of the will, he must welcome a list that contains all of what he is required to gather. But there is, or might be supposed to be, another customer for such a list, namely he who sets out to say what the best writings on that topic are. Perhaps he is the more important customer, for there must surely be a thousand who want to know what is best on the topic for every one who wants to know all that there is on the topic, and the list that satisfies him indirectly satisfies a thousand. Now no one can identify, or be sure of having identified, the best things of any sort whatever, unless he is acquainted somehow with all the things of that sort. Even if he can pick out some good ones on the basis of a partial inquiry, he cannot claim to have picked out the best ones, unless he has looked over the whole bunch. So Meyriat writes, in a discussion of the principles of international bibliographical work:[7] "*Complete* coverage is essential if the bibliography is to be systematic. The compilers of every bibliography must have access to and be acquainted with all the material published in the special field with which it deals. The bibliography may publish only a part of it, but after a process of selection presupposing knowledge of the entire material." The domain of any proper selective bibliographical instrument must be the entire bibliographical universe, and to pick out the best writings on the freedom of the will, one must have become acquainted with every one of the writings on that topic. This argument harks back to the earlier discussion of indexing;

---

[6] Richardson, op. cit., pp. 113–114.

[7] Jean Meyriat, *Report on the General Principles Governing International Bibliographical Work*, UNESCO/CUA/82 (Paris, 1957), p. 10.

for there we considered means of ensuring that those "individual thoughts that outweigh whole books, periodical articles, or chapters" should not be hopelessly lost. Now unless *all* the "individual thoughts" are somewhere identified, how can we be certain that the valuable ones have all been found? Those who come across them may not recognize their value; but how can we ensure that someone will come across them, unless we identify them all? So there are various uses that can be made of bibliographical instruments that allow collecting *all* the products of men's study and thought concerning any given topic, and the uses can hardly be considered unimportant.

Let us try to evaluate the force of these considerations.[8] Consider first the argument that a proper selection of the best things of a sort can only be made on the basis of an acquaintance with all things of that sort. It is, on reflection, hard to take this argument very seriously. We may *say* that anyone at all who discusses the freedom of the will, or any other topic, say, the building of bridges, may *possibly* have something important to say on these topics; but it is difficult to believe that we actually think this more than a remote and frivolous logical possibility. It is not in principle impossible that a writer in a magazine devoted to exhortations to piety and devotion should say something of value about the problem of the freedom of the will, or that a writer in a children's magazine should have something novel and important to say about bridges; but it is, we have to admit, extremely unlikely. We know a good deal about the conditions under which a person is likely to manage to say anything of importance about a topic, and a good deal about where people satisfying such conditions, and their writings, are likely to be found. This knowledge allows us to dismiss all sorts of possibilities as extreme improbabilities, or as *practical* impossibilities; it is practically impossible for a ten-year-old school child to say novel and important things about the freedom of the will or the building of bridges, and the bibliographer who ignored school magazines or the accidentally preserved school papers of a child would not deserve censure for his lack of systematic zeal.

[8] In *Bibliographical Services: Their Present State and Possibilities of Improvement*, The UNESCO/Library of Congress Bibliographical Survey (Washington, D.C., 1950), it is argued that "current complete national bibliographies" are necessary as a foundation for the making of selective subject bibliographies. The claim is forcefully disputed by Mortimer Taube, "Functional Approach to Bibliographic Organization: A Critique and a Proposal," in *Bibliographic Organization*, ed. Jesse H. Shera and Margaret E. Egan (Chicago, 1951), especially pp. 58–61. I shall not repeat his objections, which are practical rather than "theoretical," though no doubt the more forceful for being so.

It was argued earlier, in deciding on a definition of the domain of a bibliography, that the domain might properly include more than items actually examined; a parallel argument applies here, and indeed allows of a perfectly general extension. A person cannot absolutely guarantee that he has picked out the best items of a certain sort if he has left any unexamined, but absolute guarantees are scarcely within the power of any man to give. No one can give an absolute guarantee that he has made no mistakes in evaluation, even when he has worked as carefully as possible and has examined every conceivable candidate. Nor are absolute guarantees required of any man, or any bibliographer; to demand absolute guarantees would be to make a fanatical demand which could, in any case, not be met. A proper selection can only be made on the basis of a reasonable degree of acquaintance with the field of selection, but a reasonable degree need not be, and is not, the same as the highest possible degree. What constitutes a reasonable degree of acquaintance with a field of selection cannot, in general, be exactly specified; we cannot say that a man must have examined seventy-three percent of the items in the field, or indeed make any general statements about proportions. But that is true of most if not all other applications of the term "reasonable"; the reasonable thing is what good judgment requires, but it cannot be said that good judgment always requires the same, or any exactly specifiable sort of, thing. So it cannot be successfully claimed that the ability to collect all the products of men's study and thought on any topic is an essential prerequisite to a reasonable attempt to pick out the best of any sort of writings.

Still there is the claim that the most important items, perhaps mere fragments of discussion, *may* be forever unnoticed unless specifically identified and made available by bibliographical means. The truth of this can hardly be denied, for again it states an obvious logical possibility. Buried in the dull and dusty volumes of writings of some long-forgotten writer may be what we would now recognize to be trenchant and acute observations on the freedom of the will which, unless specifically identified, may never be found. Discoveries and proofs, insights and fragments of information, are scattered at random throughout the world's store of written records, lost or unavailable to those who could profit from them, unless identified in bibliographical instruments of some sort. How much is thus lost or unavailable, we cannot say. But no matter how much there is, it remains true that we do not bring dead or inactive knowledge and insight to life by listing in a bibliography the writing that contains it, under an appropriate heading.

The scholar who sets out systematically to read everything ever said by anyone about some topic is, I think, an imaginary figure, invented by bibliographers to justify their activities or by scholar-publicists to impress the layman. The truth is closer to that reflected in E. B. Wilson's remark[9] that though "It might be imagined that it was desirable to know everything that had been learned about the subject" of a scientific research project, in practice this is impossible and "attempts in this direction are usually a sterile waste of time." The making of bibliographical instruments which would merely list everything ever said about a topic, though not merely everything "that has been learned" about a topic, would also be a sterile waste of time, unless it were likely that someone would care to read systematically through the writings there listed, which is exactly what is *not* likely (though still more likely than that one who started such a project would finish it). The bits of fact and insight randomly scattered through the world's written records remain as lost as ever if merely listed in a bibliography, for one must have some sufficient reason for reading this rather than that writing listed, and if the important item is not marked as important, we will almost never have any sufficient reason to consult it. If the bibliographer who collects all mentions or discussions of any topic can recognize the valuable when he sees it, let him record the valuable and forget the rest; if he cannot recognize the valuable when he sees it, his work is in vain, for no one else will have the time or patience or interest to consult what he records.

Let us return to the claims of the historian and the apprentice scholar, both of whom might legitimately claim that they need the ability to collect everything on a given topic. I do not propose to question the claim, though it can be questioned. But even if we admit the legitimacy of the claim, we do not yet have sufficient reason for advocating other than the lowest degree of descriptive control of writings in general. For that a man ought to be able to find everything on a given topic does not mean that he should not have to hunt for it; and we need not propose as an aim of bibliographical policy the provision of such means of control as would either

---

[9] E. Bright Wilson, *An Introduction to Scientific Research* (New York, 1952), p. 10. Usually, he continues, it is possible to tell whether the information that the project is aimed at discovering is already available, by reflecting that no satisfactory solution of the project's problem could have been got before some fairly recently discovered technique was available.

eliminate the need for hunting or guarantee success at hunting. We could not, in any case, completely attain such an aim; but on the other hand there is no point at which we would have to stop in its pursuit.[10] It would be an intelligible policy to aim at eliminating the need for hunting as much as possible, by the ever more minute analysis of the content of all writings and representation of that content in an ever more elaborate set of organizational devices with ever more elaborate auxiliary devices. But need this be the, or a, primary aim of a reasonable bibliographical policy?

Consider two sorts of examples only. Consider the archives of an institution, the papers collected and produced in the course of the work of the institution. A person who knows only that, and where, they exist, is in a worse position than he who also knows what series or groups they are composed of, and he is in a worse position than one who has a detailed guide to the contents of each series or group. It might be proposed, as an aim of bibliographical policy, to provide the most detailed guides to the contents of all existing archives, without exception; but such a proposal would surely not be taken seriously. For archives are of most unequal value or interest, and not only is it felt that some institutional records are in greater or more pressing need of detailed guides than others, but it is felt that some records can comfortably be left without any detailed guides whatever, for the infrequent user can simply search among them until he finds what he wants.[11]

Again, consider periodical publications. A person who knows simply what files of periodicals exist, and where, is in a worse position than one who also has a detailed index to the contents of the existing files. It might be proposed as an aim of bibliographical policy, to provide the most detailed indexes, in the most conveniently cumulated form, to all the periodicals there are; but why should such a policy proposal be taken seriously?

---

[10] Schneider, op. cit., p. 52, said of his "concept bibliography" that, though it would be too difficult to make such a bibliography for any considerable subject area, "In engsten Bezirken aber ist das Verfahren nicht bloss zulässig, sondern unumgänglich." But any considerable area is a sum of narrow areas. It is the "Unumgänglichkeit" that I deny, for an area of any size. Schneider gave no reasons for the claim quoted.

[11] Nathan Reingold, "Subject Analysis and Description of Manuscript Collections," *Isis*, 53 (1962), 106–112, has interesting things to say on the increasing need for archival treatment of manuscripts, for a "group-oriented" rather than an "item-oriented" treatment. It seems to me unfortunate that management of archives and management of library stocks should be thought quite separate and dissimilar topics. It is not by accident or as a forced metaphor that scientists speak of their publications as part of "an external and permanent archive of science"; not all scientific papers are part of the stock of constantly needed "working papers," and those that are not might well be treated as other archives are treated.

For periodical files are also of the most unequal importance, some ceasing to be of any but the most infrequent interest the week after the publication of each issue, some continuing to be of interest. Not only do we feel that some are in greater need of elaborate indexes than others, there are some we feel are in no need of any indexes at all, for the occasional interested person can simply be left to search among them until he finds what he wants. Other instances can readily be furnished by the reader. If we say that a man should be enabled to find everything on a given topic, we need not say also that he should not have to work at the job or be able to do it quickly and easily.

The considerations and arguments in support of our first proposal for a general bibliographical policy are less than perfectly convincing; and insofar as they have force, they are not arguments for any particular degree or level of bibliographical control over any body of writings. A cynical member of a Supreme Bibliographical Council might say that he was not going counter to that policy in voting against the creation of new pieces of bibliographical apparatus, for he thought a bit of hunting salutary for a scholar, and the policy did not require elimination of the necessity of hunting. We might reformulate the policy so as to spell out the levels of control to be considered minimally adequate, and to discover more compelling considerations in its favor. But let us rather look at a very different sort of proposal for bibliographical policy. The first one we examined spoke of making it possible for a man to get together "results" on a given subject, and so suggested that the initiative was to come from the individual worker, who was just to be supplied with the means of doing what he wanted to do.

A quite different suggestion is contained in the claim of J. D. Bernal that "we need to be sure that every scientific worker, and for that matter every member of the general public, receives just that information that can be of the greatest use to him in his work and no more."[12] The aim of bibliographical organization he took to be that of providing each scientist, and by extension, each worker of any sort, with the information he needs

---

[12] J. D. Bernal, *The Social Function of Science* (London, 1939), p. 292. Bernal seems to have thought that it might be ensured that "all relevant information should be available to each research worker and in amplitude proportional to its degree of relevance" simply by having each worker indicate to a central distributing agency the fields of his interest, or as people would nowadays say, his "interest profile." I hope that the discussion of the notion of relevance and of exploitative control given above will have persuaded *someone* that this is not a simple matter of distribution according to "interest profiles."

at the time he needs it, and he took this to be merely a problem of distribution, a stunning oversimplification. But as there is no reason to think that a person can himself always know what he needs, or what can be of the greatest use to him in his work, it may not be wise to wait until he expresses a desire, or makes a demand on the bibliographical apparatus, and indeed it might not be wise to pay much attention to what he says about what he wants, since he may not know what he wants, and what he wants may not be what he needs. Perhaps we should envision, as the proper aim of bibliographical policy, the creation of arrangements by which the perhaps unfelt needs of scientific workers and the general public would be diagnosed by teams of bibliographical therapists, who would satisfy those needs with suitable doses of literature. For how else can we expect that the existing stock of writings will be fully utilized?

Our second proposal for bibliographical policy amounts to a proposal for the *rationalization* of work of all sorts, in so far as rationalization is possible through the most efficient use of the stock of writings. Sometimes scientists and technologists waste time in bibliographical activities that might more fruitfully be spent at thinking and experimenting; sometimes they waste time doing what others have already done. Sometimes they do less well than they might do, because they do not know of some piece of work done by another, either because they did not try to find such work, or because they could not have found it had they tried, or because they could not have been expected to try. Perhaps it is true that scientists and scholars in general tend to make better and more efficient use of available writings than do those whose work is making rather than discovering.

It is a commonplace that industrial application of scientific discoveries takes years, frequently decades, in part because those working in industrial production do not try to find, in part because they are incapable of recognizing when they do find, applicable scientific work.[13] It must be true as well that most if not all of the world's producers of goods, healers, design-

---

[13] See C. F. Carter and B. R. Williams, *Industry and Technical Progress* (London, 1957), p. 30: "If the results of basic research are to be used in industry they must cross various barriers to their communication, for often the industrial application of the research is not immediately apparent . . . a discovery published in a journal of physics in a form intended for the reading of physicists may easily be missed by chemists, and be unintelligible to them even if they find it." Derek J. de Solla Price suggests that "technology grows from technology, not from science, there being little direct connection between science and technology, though each is necessary to the other."—"The Scientific Foundations of Science Policy," *Nature*, 206 (17 Apr. 1965), 236.

ers, and professional deciders (if that is a correct description of professional managers or administrators) fail to work as well as they might do if they were to take the fullest advantage of all the knowledge and well-founded opinion that is available. It is hard to imagine that there are many people in the world who work so well that they could not profit from the study of some writings or other. At present it is costly to acquire useful information and applicable knowledge, costly in time if not in money; but perhaps it is a cost that should be fully assumed by the public, for the sake of the greater quality and quantity of output from the labor so instructed. A proper bibliographical policy would be one that was not passive, in the sense of providing the means by which those who felt a certain interest could satisfy it, but active, in the sense of supplying, unasked, those writings most likely to furnish what would improve the quantity and quality of work. This would be a policy for the most rational exploitation of writings, for the rationalization or making completely rational of the use of writings.

It would not be surprising if, at a time when even scientific work is increasingly bureaucratized and routinized, and universities can be called "knowledge factories," a policy like this should seem increasingly attractive. For if knowledge is power, power over knowledge is power to increase one's power; and if the stock of writings is thought of mainly as it represents a stock of knowledge, it is natural to propose treating it as a "resource" to be subjected to rational control, management, and utilization. Earlier I argued the primacy of exploitative control over descriptive control. This policy goes further, advocating not only that we give each person as much of that sort of power as he wants, but as much as he needs to work as well as he is capable of doing, and advocating that if he does not use that power, someone else should do it on his behalf.

We have seen how far from conclusive are the arguments that might be given in support of the first policy. What might be said in support of the second? Or does anything need to be said? It was argued, much earlier, that insofar as a man's behavior is rational, he must want to have the best textual means to his various ends. Could we not, by a simple extension of that argument, claim that every man must, insofar as he is rational, want to work as well as possible, and so necessarily also want to have supplied to him the writings that will best aid him in doing so? Does one's desire for the best available help only come into life when one sees a problem and seeks means of solving it? Is there not what we might call a "standing desire" for the best available help towards a "standing goal" of working as well as possible? If it were so, then the second policy would be a self-recommending policy, one whose desirability could be seen simply by reflection on elementary truths about human goals and the means of attaining those goals.

Unfortunately, however, the policy will not seem self-recommending to all of the workers. If it were invariably our object, in engaging in any activity, to get as much done as fast and as well as possible, or if it were invariably so in rational activity, then the policy would indeed be self-recommending. But happily we do not invariably act with that object, nor act irrationally when we lack that object. It is not irrational to potter, for instance, and the potterer might well resent the intrusion of the bibliographical therapist with his doses of literature. It is not irrational to play, and the player is not necessarily interested in playing as efficiently as possible. One might claim that neither potterer nor player is really working, so that the examples are irrelevant. This need not be so; but even one who engages in an activity for money and against inclination, and is hence indubitably working, is not being irrational in not caring to achieve maximum efficiency. Even one who engages in an activity for money and in accordance with inclination, works and likes it, is not being irrational if he cheerfully admits he does not aim at maximum efficiency.[14] Resistance to the rationalization of work, where that means work carried out with the aim of optimizing output in terms of quality and quantity, is by no means irrational; even when one does want to work "as well as possible," there are values other than efficiency in terms of which to judge performance. The policy we are considering is one that will appeal to managers of others' work, but not necessarily to those whose work is managed.

We could of course attenuate the second policy, for instance by dropping the notion of supplying individuals with what was likely to improve the quality of their work whether they asked for it or not, and making the aim that of allowing a person to discover the best means to his ends, when he wants to do so. The aim would then be that of providing exploitative bibliographical control, as the aim of the first policy was that of providing one range of descriptive control. Such general statements of policy say

---

[14] Economists and sociologists are familiar with resistance to the rationalization of work; a charming discussion of these matters is found in P. Sargant Florence, *The Logic of Industrial Organization* (London, 1933).

nothing of how much control should be available to whom, a question we must consider, though in an inevitably tentative and highly general way. But let us first rehearse some of the practical differences which might be discovered between the recommendations of a Supreme Bibliographical Council following one or the other of the two sorts of policy outlined.

It is natural, though not inevitable, that a policy stated in terms of descriptive bibliographical control should aim first at completeness in the extent of control, then at depth of analysis of the writings subject to control. It is likely that the first practical object would be to see that all writings are recorded somewhere and somehow, that nothing is outside the field of control of some part of the bibliographical apparatus. So an attempt is likely to be made to create exhaustive "national" bibliographies, recording the total output of more or less "public" writings of each country, and to create exhaustive "subject" bibliographies, recording all writings produced anywhere that are thought to fall within the scope of one or another of the conventionally recognized fields of knowledge and professional activity. The armory of "national" and "subject" bibliographies constitutes the basic conventional bibliographical apparatus, and completeness is its basic virtue, or incompleteness its basic defect. To be able to discover all the writings of a given person, or all the writings on a given subject, seem to be the conventional objectives of the conventional bibliographical apparatus, in so far as one can attribute "objectives" to such a complex mass of works produced by so many different agents under so many different conditions. When abstracts are provided for the writings falling within the various subject fields, and "annual reviews of progress" supplied for each field, the apparatus might be thought complete, or needing only enlargement in the direction of more elaborate revelation of the content of the writings recorded by means of "deeper" indexing.[15]

We might calculate increases in the amount of descriptive bibliographical control attained by estimating the "revelation ratio" of the bibliographical apparatus with respect to a given repertory of positions in an organizational

---

[15] See *Bibliographical Services* . . . (cited at note 8), p. 31: "The needs [for bibliographical services] have always been obvious. In nearly every field, there is a place for three kinds of service—inclusive indexes, more selective abstracts, and periodical (usually annual) summaries of progress." Louis N. Feipel, "Elements of Bibliography," *Papers of the Bibliographical Society of America*, 10 (1916), 177: the ideal of bibliography is "the description, in minute detail, of all the books in the world, past, present, and future, so as to be available forever."

scheme:[16] the revelation ratio is the proportion of the writings that in fact fit some neutral, non-evaluative description which are actually identified somewhere in the apparatus as fitting that description. If we consider the description "Containing discussion of the life of Keats," then the revelation ratio of the apparatus with respect to that description is the proportion of writings that do contain discussion of the life of Keats that are actually identified as such somewhere in the bibliographical apparatus. As this proportion increases, the amount of hunting and picking required to identify those writings decreases, to the advantage of the user of the apparatus. As descriptive control increased, the revelation ratio would tend to increase for each of a stock of descriptions, and the stock of descriptions itself would tend to increase. Descriptive control is not, I think, best defined in terms of the revelation ratio, for increases or decreases in control can occur without changes in that ratio for any set of descriptions, for instance through changes in the dimension of supply or time (e.g., making copies of texts available instead of mere descriptions of or references to texts, or cumulating periodically published bibliographies to make their use faster). But it would be natural to pursue the first sort of bibliographical policy by creating new apparatus that would have the effect of raising the revelation ratio for each of an increasingly large stock of descriptions, or at least to maintain the ratio in the face of the continuing torrent of publication by attempting to list everything in a few conventional ways.

By contrast, the recommendations made in pursuit of the second sort of policy are likely, though not bound, to be recommendations for the creation of what is exclusive rather than inclusive, critical rather than neutrally

---

[16] If the revelation ratio is not made relative to some stock of descriptions, or "positions," it will always equal zero, for there are an infinite number of possible positions, most of which are not represented in any repertory of any organizational device. If, on the other hand, we take all the descriptions, or categories or positions, anywhere occurring in the bibliographical apparatus, the lack of equivalence of different positions may make comparison impossible. Still, I think, the notion of the "revelation ratio" is an important one, for it is a significant feature of bibliographical instruments that, of the items in their domain, that in fact fit some given description, all, or most, or a few are identified as doing so. This is, I take it, more or less what Grace O. Kelley was investigating in *The Classification of Books, an Inquiry into its Usefulness to the Reader* (New York, 1937). The "revelation ratio" must not be confused with the degree of exhaustivity of indexing (see above, Chapter VI, note 5). A piece of writing is exhaustively indexed if all the distinguishable concepts employed are recognized in its index, which is not at all the same as giving all the descriptions that apply to the writing. Listing concepts employed is not, for example, the same as listing assertions made, and to note that the concepts of war, hell, and identity are employed is hardly the same as noting that it is claimed that war is hell.

descriptive,[17] reflecting uses to which writings can be put rather than fields of study within which they fall, directed as far as possible to the requirements of individuals and homogeneous groups of individuals rather than to the world at large; they are likely to be recommendations for the extensive and regular use of bibliographical consultants, as well as aids, rather than simply recommendations for the creation of additions to the formal bibliographical apparatus. Such a policy might be expected to lead naturally to recommendations reflecting the obvious truth that the use of bibliographical apparatus is not an activity engaged in for its own sake, that it is an activity that people will avoid so far as they can, and that it is in general more pleasant, more efficient, and quicker to ask a question of a person likely to know the answer than laboriously to seek the answer in catalogs and bibliographies. Such a policy might be pursued in the explicit recognition of *people* as part of the arrangements for control, and lead to the advocacy of formal and informal arrangements to take advantage of the peculiar versatility and flexibility of human knowledge of texts. We might naturally expect recommendations for extensive programs of translation, since the writings that would most benefit a man are frequently in languages unknown to him. We might also expect recommendations for extensive programs of rewriting, since the writings that could most benefit a man might be in effect unintelligible to him, yet capable of being made intelligible.[18] We might expect the regular employment of bibliographical counsellors as *agents*,

---

[17] George Sarton, "Synthetic Bibliography, With Special Reference to the History of Science," *Isis*, 3 (1921), 160–161: "Scientific literature is suffering from two terrible diseases which are gaining ground every day: *overproduction* and unnecessary disintegration or *crumbling*.... Many authors, not only the younger ones, take specialization to mean that any result however trifling and provisional should be the subject of a separate paper. A botanist recently remarked: 'It must be obvious to most of us that our literature is crowded with the records of incompetent investigations.' ..." The antidote proposed by Sarton was "synthetic bibliography," "selective, critical and constructive." "For example, it is a duty to denounce briefly a plagiarism or to state the futility of a book which might easily be mistaken for an important one. After having described a paper in the same way as the librarian does (perhaps less fastidiously, because we are more interested in its contents than its external appearance) one must try to appreciate it tersely asking oneself the following questions: 'What is the author's aim? What sources did he use? How did he use them? Is his work original and to what extent? What is his point of view or his bias? What are the main results of his enquiry? (quoting them if it can be done briefly). What are the main errors? (*Idem*). To what extent did the author accomplish his purpose? What other enquiries does his own suggest?' In a great number of cases it is possible to answer these questions adequately in a few lines" (op. cit., pp. 164–165).

[18] E. de Grolier, "Problems in Scientific Communication," *IBM Journal of Research and Development*, 2 (1958), 279, quotes Robert L'Hermite as advocating the systematic rewriting of scientific literature for other scientists in other fields of specialization.

reporting to workers in one area the happenings in another most likely to affect them or most likely to be of utility to them.[19] Pursuit of the second policy would naturally lead to treating the problems raised by the rapidly accelerating accumulation of writings as problems of sorting out the good from the bad, the useful from the useless, and of seeing that the good and useful fell into the hands of those to whom it was of some good or of some use.[20]

If the typical instrument of descriptive control is the exhaustive national or subject bibliography, perhaps the typical means of exploitative control would be the "special" library serving a group of scholars accustomed to talk to each other, and staffed by persons approaching the type of the bibliographical consultant rather than the bibliographical aid. If we think of such a library as one in which a deliberate attempt is made to collect all material of any description that can be of use to the workers it serves, and of the library's catalogs as just part of a complex set of arrangements whereby each worker can hope to be supplied with the best textual means to given ends, then that whole complex set of arrangements must be what we try to evaluate, when we ask about the success or lack of success of attempts to provide exploitative control. In the tests that have been undertaken to measure the performance of "indexing systems" in terms of the notions of recall and precision (or relevance) we can see an attempt to provide an analogue, for exploitative control, of the notion of the revelation ratio suggested above as a partial measure of descriptive control.[21] But the discussion of reliability in the preceding section was meant, in part, to lead to the conclusion that estimates of success or lack of success in providing exploitative control cannot hope to be other than rough and tentative.

---

[19] Carter and Williams, op. cit., p. 36: "Our analysis also suggests that the scientific middleman is very important—the research association, the technical journalist, the salesman with a scientific background, the travelling advisory officer." These are more or less casual agents.

[20] But even Sarton, who advocated selective, critical, evaluative bibliography, insisted that complete records must also be kept. "If these infinitesimal and immature publications were entirely worthless, one might throw them away and forget all about them. But the trouble is that none of them is entirely worthless; all deserve to be recorded somewhere. There is always reasonable hope of finding even in the crudest of them some precious material. Hence we are doomed to drag them along in our bibliographies, forever and ever. Another reason for quoting [?] them all is that it is only fair to give a chance to everybody and to publish at least the title of every paper however hopeless it may seem. This entirely justifies such an immense and ruinous publication as the *International Catalogue of Scientific Literature*. Time and money should not be spared to make sure that nobody be forgotten, who deserved however little to be known" (op. cit., pp. 161–162). I leave it to the reader to judge how far Sarton's remarks are meant to be ironical.

[21] See above, Chapter II, note 16, and the various writings referred to in the notes to Chapter III.

Adequacy and Bibliographical Policy   151

It is, to be sure, easy to define a measure or index of success in abstract terms, that would in theory give precise, quantitative results, if we merely grant that it is possible to rank texts as best, next best, next to next best means to particular ends. But it is quite impossible to suppose that such ranking could in practice be done "objectively," that is, done by following procedures that are both universally acceptable as appropriate and also such as to give identical or nearly identical results whenever followed accurately by equally "qualified" persons.[22] We might hope to establish procedures that involved only the identification of some set of neutrally describable characteristics of texts in order to rank texts in order of goodness as means to some end; but only a speck of reflection should convince us that there is no real hope of doing this.[23] Calling a writing the best means to an end is properly the product of a dizzyingly complex activity of evaluation, of a sort which we cannot expect equally reputable people to carry out with identical results, and cannot expect most people to carry out at all. So while we can expect stunning successes and monstrous failures in providing exploitative control to be generally recognized, we cannot hope to rank the majority of attempts in any precise order of success and failure.

Two different types of policy that might guide the decisions of a Supreme Bibliographical Council have been outlined, along with some reflections on what might be said in defense of each, and on what might be expected as the practical outcome of each. It was not intended that more than a sketch of two types of policy be given; clearly there are any number of ways of elaborating, varying, refining, attenuating, combining the two types of policy, to produce a thousand different and more precisely stated policies. It would be natural to ask: What is the correct, the *right* policy to adopt? What should in fact be the goal of bibliographical activities? Which of the thousand possible specific proposals should be adopted? I do not propose to suggest answers to those perfectly natural questions; but I do propose to suggest the character that any answer must have. Let us approach that suggestion indirectly, by considering what it would be like for the Supreme Bibliographical Council to declare that a particular bibliographical situation was adequate or inadequate.

A man may have more power than he ever cares to use, or less than he

---

[22] And since the aim of exploitative control is to provide particular individuals with the best textual means to *their* ends, agreement about the "intrinsic" merits of writings as means to ends would be insufficient even were it attainable.

[23] Compare pp. 32–33 above.

would like. If he has less than he would like, he may claim that he needs more; and it is an empty, necessary truth that a man's situation is inadequate if he has less of something than he needs. But claims to need more of a thing, if they are to be taken as other than simple expressions of desire for more, require to be justified or established, a procedure that has its own characteristic limits and rules. The most natural route of justification begins with an explanation of what the thing needed is needed for; to convince you that I need more money, or more leisure, or more sleep, I will naturally begin by telling you what it is that I cannot do for lack of money, leisure, or sleep. But not every such explanation will suffice to establish or demonstrate a need. I cannot establish a need *simply* by pointing out that there are things I cannot do that I would like to do, or that others can do. I cannot establish a need simply by pointing out that my inability to do what I would like to be able to do has in the past had undesirable consequences. I do not, for instance, necessarily establish a claim to need more bibliographical control by showing that, through lack of such control, I have failed to learn of someone else's work that would have been helpful to me, or that I have duplicated another's work by accident; all this shows is that my bibliographical situation is less than ideal, a hardly startling fact. I cannot establish a need simply by showing that my situation would be better if I had what I say I need than it is at present.

Even if I point out that my situation is very much inferior to that of others, I have proved no need, unless I can also show that I am *entitled* to as much in the way of bibliographical control as others. But this is, in essence, a political question. A man who announces that his situation is in need of improvement because as things stand he cannot do the things he wants, or "needs," to do, is asking that his interests be given equal status with, or precedence over, the interests of others: and this is a political request. Bibliographical control, it has been argued throughout this essay, is a kind of power; and requests or demands for power are, in a wide but still proper use of the term, political requests. To establish a need, one must establish a right; to establish that what I lack is something I need, I must convince you that what is lacking to me ought not be so, something that cannot be done by mere rehearsal of the facts of my situation.

It is of course true that not all talk about needs is political talk. I may correctly say that I need more power, *if* I am to do so and so; this means merely that unless I get more power, I shall not succeed in doing so and so. But the need here is an hypothetical one, and describing it entails no claim or demand; in saying that I need more power, *if* I am to do so and so, I may well be making no request at all, and saying nothing about what I want. Such hypothetical or conditional statements of need can be established in a purely "objective" way, frequently if not invariably, by reference to the "facts" of the situation, to the recognized conditions under which certain effects can be achieved. In such cases the term "need" can be eliminated entirely in favor of language neutrally describing causes, capacities, and consequences. Non-hypothetical or unconditional assertions of need, on the other hand, can be established only by proving or establishing the legitimacy of a claim. I may say I need more money, in order to winter in the Bahamas; but unless I can convince others that I deserve to be able to winter in the Bahamas, I will not be admitted to have established a need. I may say I need more bibliographical power, in order to carry out my work as well as possible; but unless I can convince others that my work is as important as, or more important than, that of others, and so deserving of as much or more support than theirs, I shall have established no need.

Finding a bibliographical situation inadequate, and hence recognizing a need, is thus admitting a political claim or demand for the amelioration of a situation. The political character of decisions about adequacy and inadequacy might be seen more clearly if we consider a possible complaint to a Supreme Bibliographical Council and a possible further policy to guide such a Council. One man's situation might be inferior to another's simply because bibliographical instruments available to the one were fewer than those available to the other, or because the latter had access to more and better aids and consultants than the former. It is perfectly easy to imagine the man in the inferior situation demanding Equality of Access, demanding, as his and every man's right, that any bibliographical instrument available to anyone be available to him, and that any amount of aid and advice available to anyone be available to him, in short, that the external situations of all men be identical. This would not make everyone's situation equally satisfactory, for the totality of arrangements and apparatus might be insufficient to allow some to do what they want, and it would still be true that differences in knowledge and ability would exist among the population. But it would remove one large factor producing differences among situations. Now does it need to be argued that a demand for equality would be a political demand, and that a decision to aim at Equality of Access would be a political decision? The demand for equality is, as it were, one of the original political demands.

The political character of a demand for Equality of Access seems obvious enough; is it not clear that all questions of adequacy that are neither purely hypothetical or conditional, or purely questions of the degree of felt satisfaction, are political as well? I will call my situation adequate if I have all I want, others will call it adequate if I have all they feel I deserve. To establish a need, I must bring others to admit that I deserve more than I have, that the things I canot do for want of power are things I ought to be able to do; but this is to convince them of what is my *due,* or of what I have a *right* to expect, and questions of rights and dues are political questions.

Still, it is likely that to many people, the political character of such demands and decisions will be invisible behind their evident economic character. For the satisfaction of a demand, or the carrying out of a policy, will cost money, and decisions on which demands to attempt to satisfy, or which policy to adopt, will be influenced if not determined by questions of cost. A cheap and very beneficial policy[24] will certainly be preferred to an expensive and barely useful one, and a loud complaint that can be silenced cheaply will be acted on before a quiet one whose satisfaction would be ruinously expensive. Now one might go further and urge than none but economic considerations *should* determine such decisions; but it cannot be claimed that only economic considerations ever *would* determine them, and in the case of the imagined policy of Equality of Access, the advocate of pure economic determination of policy would have a hard time justifying himself. But it is anyway clear that, if the decision that one policy or another be adopted requires a previous consideration of comparative costs, it also requires a (tacit or explicit) decision as to whether economic considerations shall be decisive. That earlier decision would be one to which other than economic arguments would obviously be relevant, even if one managed to ignore them. The decision that only economic considerations would determine choice would not itself be an "economic" decision, but a political one. We can have no more bibliographical control than we can afford; but how much we *can* afford, and on whom it shall be spent and in what proportions, are never purely economic questions. They are questions into the answering of which economic considerations should properly enter, where they *can* enter, but which they cannot by themselves fully

---

[24] That is, one that would increase control considerably for a considerable population, or for an important part of the population. Whether the beneficiality of a policy is to be calculated by counting each individual as equally important, or by some system of "weighting," is clearly a political matter.

answer, unless we decide to let them be decisive. But that decision would be a political one, and an odd one.

Findings on adequacy and inadequacy, on the part of a Supreme Bibliographical Council, will inevitably be political decisions, however much questions of money influence the findings. Whether the policies that guide its decisions are stated in terms of exploitative or descriptive control, or both, its decisions about who shall have how much of what sort of control will be decisions perfectly parallel in character to the decisions of other political decision-making bodies. Its bibliographical appraisers may describe the situations of particular individuals as stronger or weaker, better or worse, than those of others, or as falling short of some standard of adequacy; but setting standards of adequacy is a political matter, and deciding that a weak bibliographical position is *too* weak is a political decision. So is the adoption of one policy or another; the setting of goals and priorities in bibliographical matters is as much a political activity as the setting of goals and priorities in any other area of human action. Here as elsewhere, particular policies can be argued for but not conclusively "demonstrated," as a mathematical theorem is demonstrated, or a scientific claim supported to the point of excluding any reasonable doubt. Only the fanatic or the very naïve would suppose that the correctness of a bibliographical policy could be conclusively shown by any reflections on what people can and cannot do; no amount of abstract reflection or empirical "research" can ever establish that one policy is the only right one, or the decision to adopt one rather than another policy the only correct decision. The arguments given above in favor of two different bibliographical policies were not conclusive; and no arguments could have been so, except as they appealed to sentiments and preferences (or, if one prefers, values and principles) which no one can be compelled to share.

There is a scientific and literary patrimony, as Langlois calls it,[25] to be managed and exploited; men must decide whether they are content to record the existence of writings and store them up in repositories, or whether they wish to pursue the active exploitation of the patrimony, to provide the means of making the maximum use of the usable writings. We can, by reflection and by experimentation, make clear the possible goals and discover and test devices for the attainment of those goals; it is only by a political decision that one goal can be singled out as the "proper" goal, that it can be said who is to have how much of the power over writings, and the knowledge contained in them, that bibliographical control confers.

---

[25] Langlois, op. cit., p. 202.

www.ingramcontent.com/pod-product-compliance
Lightning Source LLC
Chambersburg PA
CBHW051615230426
43668CB00013B/2114